What have I just read? An aw[...] [...]
fortable biography wedded to [...]
through his own deeply perso[...]
look deeply inside yourself for [...]

Deon has a lot of life that he [...]
allows him to really challenge [...]
want in a coach; loud, embarrassing and too alternative.
I didn't expect to like him. Or that he would be skilled to
help me. He has humanised my leadership.

Martin Hurworth MD Harvey Water Softeners

In *My Game* Deon tells his life story whilst walking
the reader through his journey to finding purpose. He
weaves in lessons, often learned the hard way, about the
need to find purpose in our lives and offers a roadmap to
finding our own unique purpose.

Deon has a rare talent for guiding people to find meaning in their life story. He has a deep interest in helping
others discover their life's purpose and then encouraging
them to live it.

Jonathan Richards CEO BreatheHR

This warts and all biography will surely encourage others
to seek their own truth. Only by understanding who we
really are, can we really help others. The most admired
leaders are those who are there authentic selves. I am
hoping Deon's account of his own journey will encourage others to own their truth and lead by example.

It makes for some sad reading in places, but I see how Deon uses his story to channel his purpose. I admire him immensely.

Vanessa Vallely OBE MD We Are The City

Drugs, Drag, Swimming and Abuse. Not the conventional topics covered in a business book, but nothing is conventional with Deon. He uses all his experiences to gain true insight into what his Purpose is and how he can help you find yours. Can it be as easy as a formula – when you read this book you can see that it can be. A wonderful, insightful and touching book that every business leader should read.

Deon is the rarest of breeds. He is both direct and heart-warming at the same time. He uses his experience and techniques to let other people find their purpose and when they do it is truly breathtaking. The way he helps people astounds me and I am so lucky to have met him and have him help shape my purpose.

Phil Turner CEO Philharmonic

A raw, truthful and utterly compelling story forms both Deon's biography and leadership map that he invites us as readers to follow. Life is full of ups and downs, twists and turns and being an authentic leader is truly not for the faint hearted! Deon inspires us through his book to discover our own unique purpose and gives us powerful insights and a roadmap to find it.

Deon is unique! His kindness, energy and gift shine brightly and over the years have inspired thousands of leaders. I feel privileged to know and work with him!

Kate Fletcher CEO Mentor & Coach,
Board Chair & NED

Wow, I enjoyed it. I didn't know you had gone through all those challenges and I felt you were talking from your heart. Very brave.

Deon is brilliant. I attended Truth.Works. 3-day retreat which Deon runs with his colleague Emma. It just blew out of the water everything I had ever done before. Simply amazing!

What I learned from Deon has helped me in my career and private life tremendously. I continue to work with Deon as my mentor. Every-time we meet it is fantastic, the lessons I learn from him are second to none. People talk about life changing/game changing experiences, Deon is all of them very nicely gift wrapped together.

Kieran Sheahan Lecturer
Technological University Dublin

Deon has a talent; a gift is probably a more accurate description. This very personal, open and raw account of his life gives great insight and explains so much about the man he is today.

The extraordinary "King of The World" highs shrouded in the palpable upper cut punches of failure, sadness, very real fears and disappointment result in a man swimming in an infinity pool of resolve and purpose. The strength of character *that* takes shines through in his eagerness and willingness to help others be the very best and most authentic version of themselves.

Deon's generosity of spirit is infectious, impeccably timed and presented in such a way it is impossible not to throw oneself all in to his methods and madness.

He has this "thing" about him that I just cannot put my finger on. But I describe it as "getting to the heart of what makes a person not only tick, but tock too."

Sam Smith Vice President Global Solutions

My Game

My Game

The Formula for Everyday Leadership

Deon Newbronner

MOLTEN PUBLISHING

My Game

The Formula for Everyday Leadership

First published in 2018 in Great Britain
by Molten Publishing Ltd

Molten Publishing Ltd, 14 Clachar Close,
Chelmsford, Essex, CM2 6RX

ISBN 978 0 9935929 6 6 (Paperback)
ISBN 978 0 9935929 7 3 (E-book)

Acknowledgements

My Game: The Formula for Everyday Leadership has been a very special journey brought to fruition through the efforts of some very wonderful people. I am deeply grateful to my production team and all those whose enthusiasm, dedication and brilliance transformed my vision of this book into reality.

Molly you have an incredible talent.

Dedication

Ngikhona, is Zulu for I am here. I am African. This is my story, warts and all. You have one too. Use it to find, speak, and live your true purpose.

This book is dedicated to everyone who has been there for me, thank you.

Pamela, this book is because you see me. I see you. Sawubona.

Two roads diverged in a yellow wood,
And sorry I could not travel both
And be one traveller, long I stood
And looked down one as far as I could
To where it bent in the undergrowth;

Then took the other, as just as fair,
And having perhaps the better claim,
Because it was grassy and wanted wear;
Though as for that the passing there
Had worn them really about the same,

And both that morning equally lay
In leaves no step had trodden black.
Oh, I kept the first for another day!
Yet knowing how way leads on to way,
I doubted if I should ever come back.

I shall be telling this with a sigh
Somewhere ages and ages hence:
Two roads diverged in a wood, and I—
I took the one less travelled by,
And that has made all the difference.

Robert Frost

My Game

The Formula for Everyday Leadership

What if you are enough? I am enough. My story is enough. You and your story are too. I have always recognised that life and living it requires a strength to be the real me. When I have *seen me*, I am pure potentiality. I possess a capability to do, to be which seems immeasurable.

I have spent the past fifteen years helping others and myself to live purposively. When I live purposively, I realise I am *here*. The pages of this book are designed to help you do the same.

I Became Everything to Everyone and Nothing to Myself

"Make your mark, Deon. People are watching." My mother would say. I was reminded of this one weekday afternoon after school aged fourteen, I opened the fridge, to find only a packet of mini pizzas and a carton of Carnation powdered milk. I vowed my life would be filled to the brim. I was determined my legacy would never be a hollow emptiness of nothing. I would make it. There would be a purpose. I would have an impact. I was determined to do so. Fast forward thirty-three years, the fridge is always stocked.

Growing up the son of a preacher man, being in service of others is why I live. I witnessed the *in service of others* daily in my father and mother as they worked tirelessly for local communities, sometimes to their own detriment, always without reciprocity.

I remember being the child in class, particularly Geography, my fellow classmates came to for help. I knew it. Somehow, I knew how an oxbow lake formed from the meanders of a river. I knew the difference between a dry and a wet adiabatic lapse rate and the implications this had for cloud formation. But there was something else. I had an ability to see in others what they couldn't see in themselves. I was able to draw out of others the essence of them. I was able to help them see their intrinsic nature. Later, I would go on to help victims of sexual abuse become survivors by sharing my story of surviving rape and sexual abuse. I am a helper.

The truth of leadership is to know yourself, trust yourself, and be yourself; only then will you be truly trustworthy. My journey in business up until recently was about creating a community for business folk to work in and be empowered by. The irony is, it disempowered me, gradually draining me into someone who loathed the business and life and feigned interest and concern for others. This isn't me. I became everything to everyone and nothing to myself. The business failed. I kept going, only because that is what I taught myself. You are a survivor, Deon.

Tom Marshall talked about the four dimensions of intelligence underpinning leadership: cognitive, emotional, behavioural, and spiritual. The spiritual is about having a sense of belonging, and we all want to belong. We want to feel like we fit in somewhere. The emotional is being able to control one's emotions and make choices in a situation. But you can only do that once you understand your behavioural intelligence, which is understanding how these emotions manifest physically in your body and the effect it has on you and your responses to others. I think those three are the most significant compared to cognitive intelligence, which ironically is what we're assessed on as human beings our whole lives. I'm asking you to consider all four in this book.

I came to love maths in high school under the wonderfully passionate and brilliant teacher Mrs Gatley. I loved algebra and physics especially: mathematical formula and equations, having to work them out, learning formula and then applying them to problems. I guess like my *life's work*. I learn from the past and others, then apply the *formula learnt* to other aspects of life. I remember preparing for my final A-level algebra paper (well, more or less the equivalent – South African Apartheid system). On my bed would be an ocean of scrap A4 sheets of paper with hundreds – if not thousands – of quadratic equation practice examples. I was energised by the thought of doing the exam. I know it sounds a bit naff, being enthralled about algebra. It was about believing in the power of my understanding and using this knowledge in a wise and almost, dare I say, enlightened way. I got an A.

William, my six-year-old son, loves maths too. It must be in our genes. Like Mrs Gatley, William's teacher loves mathematics. When William came home from school the other day, he was so excited. He recited the nine times table, we high-fived, and I said, *"Everything has a formula, William."* Life is about key elements put together in a certain way. I used to believe life happened to me. But life is more than just hoping to fit into a pair of jeans because you used to fit into them. Life has essential components that if put together properly by using the right formula, we are happy and fulfilled. We fit our jeans perfectly.

Helping CEOs and senior business folk over the past fifteen years, I have created such a formula. A formula that when applied to every aspect of your life produces results. Yields your real meaning. It has generated a completeness for me I have never known before. It's the recipe for success. I call it, *My Game*.

$$(S + V) I = P$$

The S stands for *story and strengths*. You find what you are truly passionate about in your story. They are your real strengths, not strengths in a work context, what you are truly capable of as a human being.

The V is about your *values*. The things that are important to you. I sometimes refer to them as my standards of behaviour. You find these too in your life's experiences. Living by them brings a completeness.

Add these together and multiply them by I for *intuition*. In my experience, we place too much emphasis on cognitive intelligence. When we trust our gut, we step into a space of pure potentiality. Allow your potential to be driven by real gratitude, and what you get out of it all is *purpose*. Your truth. The essence of you. That's life.

This book is all about helping you discover the value of this formula for you. Helping you to fit into the right pair of jeans for you. It has taken me my whole life thus far to find it. This formula will fast-track you to finding, speaking, and living your true purpose.

Recently, I've decided to do a reiki course, which in my opinion is all about using your intuition to tap into your personal energy and sharing this energy purposefully with someone who needs it. Not to sound too wanky right up front in the first few pages, but I see reiki as a metaphor for life. It has, to some extent, reinforced some of the points in this book.

Acceptance Not Resignation

If like me, you have ever felt you're not good enough, or, like me, still feel at times you're not good enough to warrant the achievements you have reached, this book will be helpful. If, like me, you have asked, *who am I,* this book will be helpful. It will be helpful if you find it difficult to recognise what you are capable of. Maybe you're not sure about being able to take the next step. You know what is expected of you, but not sure how you are going to do it. You are not sure how you should *be* to continue to be the success you are. The success you know you ought to be.

There are so many books, articles and people telling us the true way to fulfilment and happiness. The best way to be ourselves. The best way to make a million. The only way to run a business. The clear path to success. All these books and stuff have one thing in common – they are about an end goal. They are about striving for something. Which by the way is wonderful and very human. They are all about what you could be.

But what if you are enough? I am enough even with my abusive past. What if within you are all the ingredients necessary, you just haven't blended them properly? You just haven't folded them in well enough. What if how you are feeling now (positive or negative) is enough? You can use your feelings in a useful, unattached way as guiding lights, sign-posts even.

What if you could live now, be now, and let go of the attachment to tomorrow and use yesterday to guide you through the present? Someone very famous said we only have the present. This book is about capitalising on how you are now. It is about the present you and the value this has for living and leading with purpose. This book will help you use your current feelings, emotions, and thinking to connect with yourself and communicate more powerfully with others. This book is a tool to help you mine what it is to be you now and cast yourself in the lead role to play life presently.

When was the last time you did something fully? Not thinking about the next thing to do. Not wondering who you might be meeting next. Not thinking through the next steps. Did something wholly.

At any given point in our lives, we are constantly looking into the future. Whether we are thinking about what time the next bus comes to assessing whether we need to allocate more resources to that project in six months.

Know your feelings, know who you are, trust yourself, and be yourself – only then will you be trustworthy.

I've Always Wanted to Do Drag, but I Never Thought I was Good Enough

When I have lived in *the now*, I haven't worried about the future. We've all experienced present-moment-ness. Growing up, I used to say, "*I can't wait till I'm eighteen*," or some other age I thought had some significance. I think it was mainly due to me wanting to be accountable for my own decisions. Dad used to say, "*Enjoy your school years, Deon. Never wish them away.*" It was his way of saying live now. Be present. I remember a time at school when I truly lived *for the now*. In the moment. Dressing up in suspenders and a bra at school and performing the song, *I'm a Lumberjack* at a prefects' assembly. Google it. It's a thing. How or where I found it, God alone knows.

So prefects' assembly in Boksburg High School in the mid 1980s was run by the prefects. Obvs. They took place on a Thursday morning. It must have been my decision to get up there and do it, and yet I remember wanting and yet not wanting to do it. Seeking validation, something we all want as human beings. Always the reluctant performer. So I found myself on stage, prancing around in front of 1600 pupils miming to this ridiculous song. I loved the stage, and I loved performing, but there was always a reluctance to perform. But when I did, I just completely went for it. That's been the story of my life.

Recently, I recorded some drag videos of me playing around with a character. I think I may have discovered Gina String. She's tall, she's thin, she's Gina String. I had this idea that I could talk about all the shit that Emma, my business partner, and I do and be dressed as Gina String. And Gina String has this sort of Joanna-Lumley-style beehive, obviously ginge, and she eats ice cream and drinks gin. I could see me doing some videos on Facebook Live and some pre-recorded ones too. Gina is an Essex gal. So in the videos, I was playing her with a sort of Essex accent, and the bit that I thought was fucking hilarious – because everything's bloody funny, isn't it? – was towards the end of the video. I stopped recording when all of a sudden, my accent became this Southern American accent. I'd gone from this real cockney, kind of broad, loose Essex kind of, *"Y'alright, luv?"* to something that was a bit more down in the deep south. WTF? But the videos are still on my hard drive. I've always wanted to do drag, but I never thought I was good enough.

This reminds me of the time I dressed up when I was married. Okay, we all had a few to drink. Or at least I think we had. I put on my wife's matric farewell dress. It was this blue fishtail number, with obvs the proverbial 1980s shoulder pads. Lovely. Matric farewell was like senior prom. So you had dinner, and there's a dance. And Jeanette had this dress, and I put it on just as a laugh, and people took the piss out of me, which is fine. I looked ridiculous. I was in the moment. It's important to do it. Live in *the now*. Not necessarily dress in drag. Well, that can be important too.

So, there I was at prefects' assembly prancing around in suspenders and a bra entertaining the masses. I loved it. But I got booed by some. But hey, I was experiencing. Playing. That's not to say I run at life full steam ahead without paying attention to what's happening. I do watch. But life, and indeed leadership, is about doing *it*. Just getting up on a stage and being you. I want to do; I will do.

I must admit though, because of my strong sense of belonging, I still proceed with caution. I approach life and decisions reluctantly. I recognise that sometimes when I conjure up the courage to do, the freedom and joy of doing is overwhelmingly brilliant. Letting go of concerning myself with the validation of others has been a life's work. It continues still to this day.

The need for approval kills freedom. Trust me, I know. I spent my entire life seeking approval until I realised it was a waste of time and didn't work anyway. The desire to get people to like me motivated a great deal of my choices and actions in early life. I mastered the art of telling people what they wanted to hear and being someone they would find impressive or just darn right outrageous. Sure, that got me the attention – all the while worrying incessantly about what others thought of me, fearing criticism, and holding myself back as a result.

I know that I am no different from you. Who doesn't want to feel that people understand them, *get* them, and at the end of it all, love them anyway? I think we all want to believe it's perfectly okay, and maybe even wonderful, to be exactly who we are. And that has to start with us, not what we do or our achievements. Nor our wealth or position in this world. Just you. You will only know your true self when you can see in yourself pure potentiality. You see you, warts and all, and you love you. It's more than respect for yourself.

In business and in life, I don't think there is anything wrong with building community. Today with everything being about the individual – me, me, me! – community is a good thing. You just have to look on Twitter and Facebook. I can't abide the self-publication, the self-adulation. But what I did wrong was thinking I could do it alone. Not really knowing how to tap into others. Believing I had to do it alone to feel I was a success. I had survived rape and sexual abuse alone. Going it alone is all I knew. But we all know businesses thrive when you cultivate the *right* relationships with the *right* people.

Life throws things at us, and sometimes things get in the way of the person we are. The funny thing about my business failures is, they have all happened for a reason. They have taught me some very important lessons about business, and I guess life too. Pay yourself what you are worth, value you. Be open to possibilities. Trust your instincts. People come and go, staying true to yourself is paramount. Don't try, just do. Plan for the future; live now. Have enough cash in the bank for at least three months. Never make the same mistakes, if you do, you're an idiot. Trust yourself and believe in you. Make time for you and family. Recognise others' contributions and praise them for it. Have a purpose because then you will have an impact. Stuff I know is so obvious, but for me it was a wonder to fail and realise these lessons the hard way.

Setting aside the business element of my business failures, the businesses failed because I didn't know how to fulfil my "why". I knew it; I just didn't know how to *be* it, to live it. I didn't know how best to execute it. That's changed. I know it, and I live it. I am it every day. I see it in the conversations I have with my son, William. I see it in the relationships I have with loved ones and friends. I am it when I am on the tennis court with my coach trying my hardest to master my Federer backhand (I do have a bit of one, a Federer backhand). I see it in the goals I set for myself. I am it in everything I do. I am not it a 100% of the time. I know I can't be. Before, being everything to everyone meant I believed I had to *be* 100% of the time. I couldn't, so therefore I collapsed. I failed. I now succeed. I now genuinely live by the poem I found at age fourteen for an art project:

Believe in yourself and in your plan (your purpose)
Say not I cannot, but I can.
The prizes of life we fail to win,
Because we doubt the power within.

This whole story of my little life reminds me of Tom Ripley (Matt Damon – the hottie) from the movie *The Talented Mr Ripley*. He said he'd *"rather be a fake somebody, than a real nobody"*. Well, I am okay being a real nobody. At least I am me.

When I started swimming at the age of three, my mother took me to RISCO swimming club. In Zimbabwe, well, Rhodesia then, Mother had to hide behind a hedge before I would go in the water. She had to hide so I wasn't being watched by her. The reluctant performer. There I was on the steps of the pool with my feet splashing about in the water. No armbands on – it was the 1970s – no frightening health and safety rules. But I wouldn't get in. *"Jeanne, the hedge!"* Mrs Palmer, my swimming coach, would shout. Mother would scurry off and lay behind a two-foot high hedge. Mother told me later how she would have to lie down so I wouldn't see her, flicking through *House & Home*. I know, ridiculously middle class.

Over the past fifteen years working with thousands of CEOs and MDs, I have noticed they too are reluctant performers. Not unwilling to step up to the plate, but reluctant to share themselves, unsure of how much to give. Suspicious of what *they* might think. How *they* might judge. Apprehensive, dare I say fearful, of who they truly are, and unknowing of the impact they could really have. Instead, they have, to a large extent, auto-piloted their way through their career. Reluctant to show their true emotion and vulnerability. Being authentic means being vulnerable. It means letting different people see the different facets of you, trusting the different version of self. And if *they* judge that's completely about them.

There have been times in my life where I haven't known if I am Arthur or Martha. I stand for many things. I believe in differing perspectives of life and self. Ever felt like you don't know who *you* is? Spent your life playing so many different roles in work and in life?

As an actor, I have played many roles in my life. But as an actor, I have known who I am, the actor. I have known my purpose and understood my story. I just wonder then how do we as leaders know who we are? How do we find our truth and live it? How do we live with purpose, leave a legacy and have the impact we want? How do we fill up our fridge?

I have always been a bit of a slow starter. Although Mrs Palmer always told my mother, "*Deon has a natural ability.*" Maybe I've used this as an excuse to not do.

On a blistering hot day at school – I must have been about sixteen years old – I was on the starting block. Cap

14

on. Knees wobbling. And very noticeable. I've always had these very noticeable knees, mainly because I have such skinny legs. Imagine this sixteen-year-old ginger kid with knobbly knees, skinny legs, poised on the edge. Always on the edge. On the cusp of something. Moments before greatness. Within grabbing distance. I was on the edge of the pool, oblivious that this race would be a metaphor for the rest of my thirty-one years.

"*On your marks!*" I was focused. The sun was beating down on me. Sweat was pouring off me. I was on the edge of heaven. That crisp, cool water glistened in the midday heat. I was determined. One single-minded intention. No looking left and right. No movement at all. Fully present. I could hear my heart beating. It was surprisingly slow and gentle. I knew what I must do. I knew what others wanted from me.

There was no noise from outside my head either. Nothing cluttering my mind. I could see the other edge. The hundred metre butterfly, that's all. Easy. I had spent years – well, it seemed like years – getting ready for this. I believed I was on the cusp of winning. I knew I was. Mrs Palmer believed in me. Winning the victor ludorum, "the winner of the games" would be my crowning glory. Hey, I'd be as good as my nemesis; my older brother Allan. The story of my life, the comparisons with anyone and everyone. The near-missus, close but no cigar. Would this be the same? Would I do it? Was I fast enough? Mr Doubt. Always with a steely determination to keep going. Never giving up. Mrs Belief. Although Dad used to stay, "*No stickability, Deon,*" fuck that!

Then, a huge crack of the starting gun, and I careered off my block into the crisp, cool water. Before I knew it,

I was up on top of the water, skimming along like a motorboat. I could feel I was synchronised – my arms and legs flowing perfectly. There was only water, breath, and movement, my heart beating like a mauri bongo drum. Thump, thump, thump. I was ahead, leading the pack.

I looked to the right. Noooooooooo! My arms began to ache. Heavy like someone was pushing down on them. They didn't appear to rise above the water.

I couldn't get them up and over. Rhythm? I'd lost it. What was happening? Why had I looked right? Why didn't I stay focused? Present? Swimming my own race?

I was always getting distracted. Always wanting to hold on. Moving focus away from what I saw inside me and grabbing hold of stuff and experiences I found myself in, losing traction, and finally giving up. Maybe Dad was right. Mr Doubt.

I looked right again. I saw him, Jack. He was now half a body length ahead of me. I pulled harder and faster. The pain in my arms was so intense. They were numb, yet nail-penetratingly painful. The vice-like grip on my chest from the water took my breath away. I pulled up alongside Jack. We were neck and neck. If I just reached, I could do this. Reach. Fingertips inching towards the edge in split-second time. I felt the side of the pool with my fingertips.

I came up from the water and looked around. Jack was right there. I looked up at the time-keeper for my lane. There used to be a time-keeper for each lane. Remember, it was the early 1980s, no digital pad imbedded into the pool side. *"Excellent time, Deon. Well done."* I nodded. All I wanted to know was did I beat him? Was I the "winner of the games"?

Jack beat me by a hundredth of a second that day. Jack won the victor ludorum. He was also selected for Currie Cup, South African nationals. Without purpose, there is only self-judgement and criticism which leads to doubt and attachment.

You hear all this business speak that tells you *it's not about surviving, it's about thriving,* but I think it is about surviving, and I've always had a strong sense of that survival. I think it comes from the time of Gary and the sexual abuse. I felt I had to do it on my own, and I chose to do it on my own. I chose not to talk to anybody. That was not about the people around me. I'm not saying I couldn't talk to them; I just chose not to. I chose to figure out how to survive on my own.

So when businesses were failing, when each one of them failed, I always believed that I would go on. I always believed that I would find a way. And even with Pitch Perfect Club coming to an end at the later part of 2016, beginning of 2017, I always believed that from the ashes the phoenix will rise. And it does. As long as you're present, tap into your intuition, pay attention to what's going on around you, understand who you are and your values, know your strengths and story, you are able to survive. Detach yourself from the experience. I am not the experience. I am me. See whatever challenges you face and notice them from a distance. I learnt this useful tool of detachment during the years of sexual abuse. I learned to live around the edges of my life. Not the nicest process of discovery, but useful now. I know that's what's got me through some of the shit that's happened in my life.

The guilt and shame I have felt perpetuated a world that was confusing, impenetrable, and frightening.

However, living my purpose does not remain static; it has changed. Much like the wonder that is this life, there have been ebbs and flows to it. Ups and downs with many losses and many mistakes that cannot be undone, and yet I continue to live with purpose. My intention is that you read this book with a desire to find your purpose, to sing your song in the chorus of life. My intention for this book is that you'll find it a resource to help you tap into you. You have a deep reservoir of strength, of courage to live the life you know you ought. I know I needed help, and I got it not only from others but importantly from myself.

It's about the journey and not the end itself. The memories of that hundred fly race have stayed with me. I got all the praise in the world from the people I loved. But I didn't win the prize. Close but no cigar. The thing is, I never give up living. Fuck, I sometimes feel like giving up. A lot. But never have. There is always another time, another opportunity. Fast-forward thirty-one years, I see business and life much the same way as I did swimming that race. We can get so close to being *the* one, we want it so badly, grabbing at *it*. We keep searching, looking forward, and yet sometimes we feel like we may never get to *it*. I had forgotten the strengths and values that lie within me. What about living our own truth? Do you live purposefully?

We see so much stuff reported in the news. Hear so much information about incidents through social media. Wasn't it Thomas Gradgrind in Hard Times that said "*facts alone are wanted in life*"? Arguably, we are screaming out for accurate information. We all seem to be drowning in bad data and misinformation, the fake-news era. And sometimes we feel we cannot believe it all.

And so we question its validity. I know I have. Currently, where there is so much accessible information and bad data, I wonder to myself what is truthful? What is real?

The illusory truth effect has been flying around the world of psychology since 1977. But recently, more and more evidence has arrived to back it up.

The more you repeat a lie, the more people will believe it to be true. I knew as a kid the more I wanted to convince someone of something entirely untrue, the more I needed to repeat it. Over and over. I was a master at it. I wasn't abused; Gary loved me as his son. I kept telling myself *it* didn't happen. Consciously fuelling my daily struggle of lying to myself and others. Perpetuating a fantasised reality. I believed my lies. I told myself often enough.

The illusory truth effect is the idea that if you repeat something often enough, people will slowly start to believe it's true. Sounds about right, considering all the times we've blindly trusted an old wives' tale or a much-retweeted factoid. But in recent studies relating to the illusory truth effect, it's been found to be much stronger than we imagined. Because it turns out that even if a person has prior knowledge disproving a lie they're being told, they'll *still* believe the lie if it's repeated enough.

We live in a world where success is ultimately defined by what I have achieved – what I have, my perceived status in the world, the people I know, the wealth I have created, the degree of influence I have, the number of followers, likes, and shares I get on social media. All of this is imaginary, right? It isn't real. Yeah, sure, having the fancy house in the south of France is. Or the Austin Martin in the drive is too I guess. But the perceived possession of success – the status – isn't real. Knowing yourself, trusting yourself, and being yourself is real.

I can prove it. Recently, the business I was running went bust. My business partner, Emma, and I had made some terrible mistakes. Wrong decisions about people and definitely bad decisions about purpose. Not living our truth. So, we went bust and had to let people go. Awful. Suppliers not getting their dues. It took a good six months to sort. I am still up to my ears in debt. Guilt and shame are still raw. Having said that, I have a family to support and must keep going.

In January 2017, I landed a great contract with a large global corporate client. Emma and I were about to fly out to the US to deliver the work. It was our purpose: helping senior people get to grips with their story and their truth. Helping us all find, speak, and live our purpose. It's what we do. Emma posted her excitement on social media. Oh dear. Oh no. That den of untruths and misinformation. That hole of darkness where people say stuff, and where that stuff gets misinterpreted. The global Chinese whispers.

I believe Emma's intention was to feel some positivity. To help her (and us) move on a little from the hell of the past six months. What happened next neither of us expected. Emma received a barrage of insults and abuse from people via email. One in particular asked how we could do this when we owed them money. And in a way, they were right. But little did they know that this particular contract was just enough to allow me to put food on the table and keep a roof over our heads. Their perception of us was wrong.

My simple point is, we strive for external signs of

success, when all we need do is look inward and know ourselves, trust ourselves, and be ourselves, not the roles we play online or off-line. *That* is real success.

Think about it. Ultimately, we want to be liked, right? We are needy. We put stuff out on social media. Why? Because we believe we have a voice. And rightly so. But we also want to get likes and smiley faces. And shares. We want validity. I laugh to myself whenever I hear someone say, "*I don't like needy people.*" As social animals, we all have needs. When I am annoyed with someone's apparent neediness, it's likely I don't like that I yearn for this need to be met in myself.

On the positive side, my needs are the drivers of my success. My need for attention helps me to succeed as a writer, business owner, and public speaker. My need for recognition drives my desire to do good work. My need for control helps me take charge of projects and run a successful business.

Therefore, I am needy. Everyone I know is needy. We all want to be seen, understood, feel cared for, and feel valued. Tom Marshall describes this as the spiritual dimension of intelligence underpinning leadership. Yet, this reality doesn't have to control our feelings, thoughts, and behaviours. You can become the master of your needs instead of letting them control you.

Over the years, my comparative judgments have blocked me from seeing what I can learn from myself and seeing what I can learn from others and the situation. On a simple level, it has stopped me from having conversations that could improve my life, my business. My reactions to unmet needs have stopped me from feeling content. So do we say and do what we know to be right?

Or do we say and do what we believe others want to hear from us? Letting go of what others might think has been a huge weight lifting off my shoulders. But *the letting go* is a life's work. *They* think what they think, God bless them. There are people who will love me, and there are people who will not like me at all.

I like to think about all this as if I were watching a movie, noticing my reactions with curiosity, respect, and compassion. I hear the voices in my head. And there are plenty. The voices don't have to be my demons; they are my angels, my teachers to help me grow.

I Have Always Wanted to Do A Good Job

I felt very isolated as a teenager. I would do my school work, but I wouldn't be committed to it. My friend and partner in crime, Brendan, told me about the Johannesburg School of Speech and Drama, and I wanted to go. It was a boarding school, and I thought that would be brilliant. I could go to boarding school and get out of the house and its horrible atmosphere. But my father said no, so I never went. And I resented that. It was the one thing that really fucked me off as a teenager.

Once I'd finished high school, I went to university. But I didn't go to university to study what I wanted to do; I went to study something because my dad said I should become a teacher. So reluctantly, I went. The best bit about being at university was the drama club. I became the student representative of the drama committee. I won the best actor award that year in the inter-college drama festival, and I got a real taste of what I thought I could be. It was freeing being a version of myself others didn't see every day.

Dawn Denton, a very dear friend of mine, and I did a lot of sketch shows together. Although I have no memory of much of it. She talks about us doing this really bad comedy sketch. We were the only two English speaking people in this Afrikaans theatre festival, and we did this really bad sketch taking the piss out of Adam and Eve. I have no recollection of this, nothing whatsoever. She said we were booed off stage because Afrikaans people in general are quite religious, and we were being blasphemous. Terrible. But fun, if only I could remember.

That was the year Mandela was released. I still remember our friend Trudy running up to us one Saturday afternoon frantically waving the newspaper in her hand with a headline, *Mandela is Released*. We were on the perfectly manicured lawn in front of our whites-only residence in our whites-only College of Education where we were learning lines or something. She yelled, *"Mandela's been released! Mandela's been released!"* Dawn and I in unison went, *"Mandela? Who's Mandela?"* which for me epitomises how isolated you were if you were a privileged white South African. The media was so closed down. You didn't get to see what was going on. It was such a policed state. But also part of it was not wanting to know. We were too caught up in our own way of life, on autopilot almost. I learnt the hard way to open myself up, to be aware and be present about what's going on.

The funny thing is, I was always aware of how I felt about what I was doing and thinking, but I wasn't necessarily aware of the situation itself, especially growing up in South Africa. I have a lot of guilt and shame about that. I lived such a sheltered life. The people abroad knew more about what was going on in apartheid South Africa than I did. But now when I think back, there were people my age in our country that did something about it. They made a difference. I didn't.

I have always wanted to do a good job. Always wanted to make sure I checked-in with myself, checked-in with others too. The latter can be a little confusing and at times, downright debilitating. Using others to check-in on self-progress allows Mr Doubt to walk back into my life. Self-reflection ushers Mr Doubt right back out the door. Turn around, I don't want you any more. I have Gloria Gaynor singing away in my head writing that. But it's true. When we try to become everything to everyone, we become nobody to ourselves. The trick I have learnt is to first become somebody to myself. As a result, I will be someone to others. It's like I walk this invisible line between the me I see and the me I want to see.

It's important to get valuable timely feedback. As a leader, you don't get much of it, right? So why not do it for yourself? You know time is a great healer, that over time things don't always seem that bad. You put things in perspective. But, have you ever noticed that time can fundamentally alter your outlook on life? Think back to the last time you had an argument with a colleague or a stranger.

I recently called a certain car dealership. My new car had broken down a day before Christmas. There we were, stuck on the M4 leaving London. I needed a courtesy car. The operator on the phone just wasn't listening to me. At the time, I was fuming, and for hours afterwards I was thinking of all the clever things I could have said. The aftereffects of the argument ruined my whole morning. It's only later I haven't felt irritated by it any more. And a great deal of the time, I hardly remember it at all. The sting has gone out of my turbulent emotions. The event still happened, but I remember it from a different perspective.

My father and I had quite a peculiar relationship. He did the best job he knew how to do. He was criticised a lot by his father and made to leave school. The irony is he too wanted to go to art school. He was an incredible artist. I remember watching him draw these almost photo-like pencil sketches of steam engine locomotives. He was fascinated by trains.

Dad relived my grandfather's parenting approach. My father used to say I was lazy. When my father used to say things to me, I'd think, *Well okay. I'll be that then*, which is why I never put a label on William. When your parents tell you something often enough, you begin to believe it. My father told me I was lazy, had no stickability, and was a 'slapgat', which is an Afrikaans word that means lazy arse. So I perpetuated that.

My father was so caught up in the church. His belief that the life hereafter was the most important and we're only here temporarily consumed him, so in my teenage years, he was never around. He was focused on that. He would have great relationships with other people and other people's children in his church, and I resented that. I don't any more. You'd expect me to have such an aversion to Christianity and religion because of my father, but I don't because it's my truth, my connection, my spirituality. It doesn't need to be tainted by my relationship with my father or the lack thereof.

He encouraged me and Jeanette, my ex-wife, to come to his church, and we did, and I could see him having these relationships with other people in the church, and I just resented that. The minister's wife at the time took it upon herself to pray for me because I had *unnatural feelings*. And when I told my father I was gay, he too wanted to pray for me.

When my mother died, I called him, and it was the

first time I'd spoken to him in maybe twelve-thirteen years. I called him out of duty to tell him, but I also called him because I wanted him to be kind and console me. He was my dad, right. I guess I had a high expectation of how he would perform. He failed miserably. He said let's pray for her, but I didn't want to pray. He told me she'd gone to a better place and started to preach about the life hereafter and all of that. All I wanted to hear was, "*I'm sorry, son. I'm sorry for your loss.*" I wanted him say things like, "*Your mother and I had difficulties, but she was a beautiful woman*" or whatever. There was a huge expectation on my part that there would be something like that from someone who had never expressed that kind of affection. Projecting our hopes onto others can be at worst disastrous, at best naive. Often, our expectations of others are misplaced.

Changing your perspective can transform your experience of life. Living my purpose has certainly changed mine. Time is a great healer, but so is living your purpose. The trouble is, as in life, if you rely solely on outside circumstances to change in order to be happy, you have to wait a very long time. If you are constantly seeking feedback on your performance, you end up not knowing how good you can be. You measure your success and self-worth through another's eyes. I am not saying don't get feedback. We're all needy and want recognition. Pay attention to the degree to which you seek the "approval of the audience or seek feedback from those around you.

We can get easily caught up in doing mode – getting the feedback from others and making changes. Make a shift in your perspective and feed-forward on yourself. It is an alternative to fuelling the *doing* mode and entering the *being* mode. When your reference points are internal, your measure of success is yourself, and not where others believe you lie in relation to them. It allows you to see your mind in a way that's not distorted by another's reality. You begin to experience the world directly. You see any distress you're feeling or happiness you're experiencing from totally new angles, and you handle life's difficulties very differently.

I have found I am able to change my internal landscape irrespective of what's happening around me. I am no longer dependent on external circumstances for my contentment with what I have done. I use my own values as my standards for measuring the success of my talk or presentation, or the way I am being moment to moment when speaking.

Henry, a brilliant leader of a very famous global drinks brand, asked for my help recently. We met in this bar/restaurant that had a separate function room. *"Deon, I need help with being concise. I talk too much and lose my audience. They look bored. They fiddle with their phones and look down."*

I thought to myself, do I tell him that maybe these people he's using to assess his effectiveness are not visual processers? Or should I get him to try it? I obviously went with the latter. I got Henry to go to the bar. We were in a lovely traditional Dutch pub in Amsterdam. Love that city. I wanted him to recognise the power of self-observation. Of being able to notice, for himself, what he might want to keep doing, or what he might want to change. At the bar, he was to ask for some bottled water (it was the middle of day and we were working. No need for gin – yet) and then have a conversation with whoever was serving him and notice what he thought and/or did whilst talking to them. I too was present, observing.

When we got back to the function room, we exchanged feedback. *"Henry, what did you notice?"* Henry reluctantly said, *"I spent the whole time in conversation, thinking about what she was thinking. Whether she was listening."*

When we use others' perception and their apparent non-verbal and verbal cues as our measure of success, we lose sight of who we are. Why we are there. Our purpose. We must change our perspective and measure success by our own internal compass. Then time becomes a great healer.

"And so what did you do because of that?" I asked.

"I became more and more self-conscious," Henry said with an almost frightened look on his face. *"I was uncomfortable. I wanted to stop. Get out of there. I tried harder to speak to her, and I started to act. I was acting interest in her and what she was saying back to me."*

I looked at him, *"You become something you are not. You became untruthful. Fake?"*

There was a pause, *"Yes, I did. I noticed how I became so fixated on that, I lost why I was speaking to her."*

If, like most of the leaders I work with, you want to make your presentations and public speaking better, you want to make your interactions with others better, if you want to build a strong foundation for building trusting relationships, then you need to take stock. And dare I say, be less concerned about what others are doing. Now, I am not saying ignore the obvious signs, but don't be driven by what you might be interpreting from those signs. Using feed-forward can really help with this. When we observe without judgement, we create space to intuitively alter how we think, feel, and behave.

I am reminded of the book, *The Inner Game of Tennis*. Ever read it? If not, you must. It talks about us all having a *Self 1* and *Self 2*. *Self 1* is your conscious mind. It judges, assesses, and analyses. When we don't do what we intuitively know is right to do, *Self 1* tells us off. I see my *Self 1* in many aspects of my life, not least of all in my own tennis game. Watch the ball, Deon. You're not getting the right footwork in place before taking the racquet back. You are lifting your head when you are hitting the ball. But *Self 1* appears in other aspects of my life too, like running the business. Telling myself off for not saying things a certain way when I am public speaking and for not conducting that meeting in the best way. I see it as the inner critic. Always concerned with making it happen. *Self 2* on the other hand, is instinctive. It's intuitive. When we trust ourselves to do what we know is right, we are tapping into *Self 2*. It is about *letting it happen*. When we observe without judgement, we step into the freedom of *Self 2*, which in my opinion is flow. It is *being* mode. For far too long I have allowed *Self 1* to drive my decision-making in business and life.

My mother always said to me, "*Life, Deon, is like being invited to a posh dinner. When you want something, and you find yourself getting excited about it, ready to do anything and everything to get it*" – which she believed was the equivalent to reaching across the table and grabbing – "*just remind yourself, Deon, that's bad manners. Wait your turn. Your time will come.*" I take this principle further into helping clients become more grateful for themselves. Self-gratitude feeds an understanding of your choices and of who you are. Mother would say savour the taste of things at dinner. Enjoy it all. Enjoy the present moment. How many times have you just been fixated on the result? How many times have you stood up in front of a client in a pitch or in front of your team and just talked at them to get to the end? Being thankful for your choices in each moment can lead you to living your truth. Being thankful cultivates an ability to pay more attention to the impact you are having.

I know when I have used feed-forward when reflecting on my life, I have a very different view of the past and see the future in a new light. I let go of my mate doubt and say hi to my pal belief.

Alison too recognised this in herself recently. Alison is a powerhouse CEO of an international FMCG business based in the US. She and I have been working together for near on twelve months. Alison speaks globally, and after every speaking opportunity, she and I feed-forward. I remember an occasion when I went to watch her in London, and we talked afterwards. Even after twelve months, Alison's first words to me were, "*What do you think?*"

I said, "*What do you feel you did well?*" As humans, we all tend to have what I call a negative-bias. We focus on what we didn't do so well. What we got wrong. How we must change. What isn't working.

Feed-forward and my work is to help you focus on the good stuff you do, whilst recognising the elements you need to improve. And at the same time, helping you see what you ought to be thankful for. It's a great simple tool.

The Practice: Feed-Forward

Feed-forward is based on three clear steps. Use

feed-forward to observe yourself. When you give yourself feedback or you seek feedback from others, it can sometimes come across like *Self 1* judgement. Looking back is not going to help you progress as a public speaker and presenter. Without wishing to sound too much like Lady Macbeth, what's done is done. Feedback focuses on the past. Feed-forward is all about your future as a great public speaker, presenter, leader. Person. Let's take a walk through the steps.

Step 1 – The first step is all about asking yourself what you did well. You need to give yourself space to say, *Yes, that worked. Yes, I did it.* It might be appreciating particular aspects of your last presentation or talk that went well for you. It could be how you altered the pace of your delivery or how you relied on fewer slides. Or how well your intent worked. It is important to be truthful.

Step 2 – Ask yourself what you will do next time to change things and improve. But remember, it's not about what you did 'wrong'. This step focuses on potential solutions and improvements, not on the past problems. So in essence, it's about questioning what you will do the next time you deliver this talk, or a similar presentation, to improve. It could be thinking about the possibility of using a different personal story to get more of an audience reaction or deciding to spend more of your allotted time to hit home the parting shot of your talk.

Step 3 – Here comes the rub...this is when you need to ask yourself, *What am I grateful for? What should I give thanks for?* It could be thinking about being grateful for feeling confident before you started even though it may have been the first time you were delivering some new material in your presentation, or it could be simply showing gratitude for the level of audience engagement you felt. It can be anything. Again, what is important here is being truthful.

Sometimes the third step can be quite tricky to get used to. But ultimately, step three is about cultivating a sense of happiness with self. There is a lot of stuff out there on the internet about how to do this. Some come across as being a bit corny. But it has more than a bit of truth in it. Actually, it has a lot of truth in it. And let's face it, why wouldn't you want to create a sense of happiness with your presenting, public speaking, or how you are communicating with others?

You Shouldn't Do Something Just Because Other People Want You To

I had to join the army because conscription was compulsory for white males in apartheid South Africa. I believed I had no choice. I did. In high school, we had to register. Even at the age of sixteen, or it might have even been fifteen, you had to register. But at the time, I didn't think anything of it. I was so naive and blinded by what was going on in South Africa. I was so sheltered. I just thought this was what people did.

We lived in such a policed state that it even went as far as teaching us a subject at school called MP, which was *moral preparedness*. It was subtle, at times underhanded and manipulative. The boys had to go to the field and march, and girls had to go and do needlework. Moral preparedness: prepare you for this policed state, to fulfil the role that you ought to fulfil. A woman's place was supposed to be at home in the kitchen, and a man's place was out earning money or killing people. *Defending freedom*, the freedom of the oppressors for which I was seen as one with my white privilege. And this perpetuated my narrow-minded, bigoted, homophobic mind set.

Growing up in this environment where my parents weren't activists, I fell into line. I believed I had no choice. I lived as the state intended me to. We have, and you have nothing, not even your dignity. I was determined to make conscious choices that served me. I wanted out. Out of the army, out of the system, out of the country.

I have noticed over the course of a day, I make numerous choices in business and in my everyday life. At the conscious level, I make hundreds, if not thousands, of choices every day. At the unconscious level, I make an incalculable number of choices daily; breathing is a significant one. When I choose to focus my energy to make as many of my decisions consciously, I have noticed I maximise my ability to pursue what I love with purpose and a sense of curiosity. I possess a *yes...and* attitude. I create positive change.

For example, on mornings when I wake up and choose to have a good day, I have prepared. I meditate the night before. In the morning, I apply some self-healing reiki, I eat a healthy, good breakfast, and I set about not diving in to review my tasks for the day. Well, not immediately. I do something, even if for just five minutes, that I love. This morning, William and I played *Top Trumps*. All these conscious choices over time become an unconscious consciousness, and they changed my internal environment.

I liken these conscious choices to the third number-one rule of improvisation. In improv, *yes...and* means accepting ideas, thoughts, and choices and building on them. The power of *yes...and* has had a profound effect on my approach to life and business. I open up to the possibilities. By the by, the first number-one rule is make everyone look good. The second number one-rule is be spontaneous.

Accepting offers, making conscious choices with a *yes...*

and attitude, fuels *right* choices, and is the foundation of all relationships. What is flirting but a way of saying *yes, I want you, I like what I see.* Let's face it, when we want to *get jiggy with it*, we adopt a *yes...and* strategy. It is all about seeing the opportunities and making the *right* choices. In business negotiations, it is all about finding the solution that meets all parties' needs – that each side is willing to accept. The sales process consists of getting the customer to say *yes* to whatever it is you are selling.

My choices are statements about my priorities. They really are my values. Making conscious choices has opened and closed doors for me, all the while driven by mindfully living my purpose. It is the driving force behind the conscious choices I make, asserting an active unconscious consciousness and thus taking control of my own destiny.

So I registered for the army at fifteen or sixteen, and then I deferred it while I was at school. I continued to defer it while I was at university, but when I finished, I couldn't defer it any more. So I went to the army, and I fucking hated it. I wanted out. I tried every single thing I could to get out of it. My brother thought it was great that I was going because he'd loved it. It was another one of those situations where someone (my family) was telling me what to do.

When it came to making some significant, conscious life choices, being on the right side of the law in a policed state presents its perils too. Certainly, my hardship was not at the same level of the majority of citizens in South Africa. I didn't want any part of it. *If I can't get out of this legally, I will do it my way.* Oh, it will make you into a man, people would say, including my family.

I was originally called up to go to a place called Upington in the Northern Cape, which was the arse end of nowhere. I was called to join the infantry, but I knew I would likely end up being bullied there (raving queen trying her hardest to be straight), so I took it upon myself to find the easiest route. Much of my life, I've tried to find the easiest route. But this time, I had a purpose. It was my way of objecting, making a stand. I possessed such resolve and determination. When my purpose has been clear to me, and I have lived it, everything doesn't just fall into place, but it gives me meaning and direction. I want to do. I am being.

My choices determine my destiny. I constantly make choices in business and in life. We all do. Unfortunately, I, like most entrepreneurs, have made significant decisions on auto-pilot. Instead of consciously evaluating the direction and results I have wanted to achieve, I have jumped ahead, taking action. The businesses have failed. In contrast, those of us who consciously guide their organisations forward, do so by establishing clear business objectives and plans before moving forward. I know now the first step in everything I undertake is to consciously choose what I want. Do you do this for yourself?

When I seek to make a difference, it is an intentional choice. I am living my purpose. I structure my priorities to create change. That change leads to identifying areas that can be eliminated. I know then I have the impact my heart desires. This comes from the choice of deciding what is most important to me.

When I realised the Medical Corps was in Pretoria, which was close to where we lived in Johannesburg, I decided that was where I would go. It was accessible, unlike

Upington, which was about eight hours away. I'd also heard it was easier. I convinced myself that because I was in St John's Ambulance, I would be good at medic duties. So I wrote the army a letter explaining that I was in the St John's Ambulance and Scouts, and I should go to the Medical Corps. And then I got a letter being called up to go.

Conscious choice is nothing without curiosity. Children are born with an innate curiosity about the world, themselves, and their environment. William spent most of this morning before school making coffee for the adults in the house. Obvs in between playing *Top Trumps* with me. He was curious about how the coffee machine worked. The machine that Daddy uses every morning, which makes Daddy perk up. Think about it. A baby takes joy in gazing at their foot as it moves, or the toddler who waddles across the room, checking back to see that the adult in its life is still there to protect them. Do you encourage that curiosity in them? Have you encouraged that curiosity in yourself? Or do you just ignore it, squelch it, or worry about it?

I have spent my life consumed by self-comparison. A *yes...but* mind set. An agreeable but closed-down approach to life, to leading. The ability to be curious, open, and accepting drives useful conscious choice. It drives open the heart into a freedom no prison can contain.

I knew I had to go to the army. I couldn't become a conscientious objector. I'd be picked up by the military police and taken to one of those camps. If you flouted the law, that's where you'd end up. There was one of those camps near Boksburg North. I'd travel to school on the bus, and it would pass this camp, a prison camp. I recall one afternoon on our way home, it was stiflingly hot. Driving past the camp, we saw men outside, but within the barb-wired fencing, digging in the hot dirt. One older boy from one of the Afrikaans schools on the bus shouted out, (in Afrikaans) *"Look there! That's where you go when you don't do your duty."* Then he laughed and pointed and banged on the bus windows at the men. And reluctantly, I had to do *my duty*.

I can still remember the day I went. I was scared shitless. My mother and brother took me by car to Pretoria to this huge warehouse, and there were buses and buses of all these young men. These days happened often, daily, monthly all year round.

I was so frightened that I was filled with tears, much like a child on their first day of school. What the hell had I done to end up here? What the hell were my brother and my mother making me do? But it was the law. I had to go.

It's quite suffocating even now thinking about it. I was about to go into a system that had perpetrated so many crimes against people. I was about to get ready to support this policed state, fulfil its purpose. And I thought, *fuck that. I don't want to do that.* And maybe that was my little rebellion. After all, I did everything I could to get out of it.

I lived such a sheltered life that I found it strange that there were troops and platoons of non-whites in the army. Now, thinking back, I understand that of course there were because some people believed in the government of the time. There were women there too.

We were taken to where you get your uniform, and the uniform was this brown, khaki thing, and I really look shit in brown, although with my burgundy beret on

I think I looked all right. Gay, gay, gay! There's a photograph of me in my browns picking up Jeanette, and I'm saluting in a really camp way. I looked quite fit but gay.

After that, we were taken to our dorm, and basic training started, and so did getting up at two o'clock in the morning, ironing your bed, polishing your boots, and all of that. We also had to go through a series of medical checks for the first week to get our health classification. I knew I needed to not be a G1K1. If you were a G1K1, it was a licence to be completely fucked around because you were perfectly healthy, and they could do whatever they wanted with you. I wanted a G6K6, which was an honorary discharge on the grounds of health. So I developed asthma. I think I probably did have asthma, but all of a sudden it became something significant. I had all these asthma attacks because of the dust, and I had to go to 1 Mill, 1 Military Hospital, which was this huge hospital right on our barracks. In that week, I did everything I could from asthma attacks to collapsing on the parade ground to dizzy spells, and of course they couldn't find anything wrong with me. I got a G3K3 classification, which was restricted duties.

Basic training lasted about three months. And after it, we were sitting on the parade ground, and they were asking for volunteers to do different jobs around the camp. They needed people to work in the canteen, and I said I worked in a restaurant and knew how to deal with money and stock and everything like that, and so I went. I worked in the canteen for a whole year. In Afrikaans they called me a 'kantien tiffey', which was canteen little server. Its sounds rather like a derogatory gay term. Oh the irony.

I managed to get myself a 'sleep out' pass, which meant I could go home every night. I would hitchhike to get home, but you weren't allowed to put your thumb out if you were in the army. You just had to walk, and people would pick you up because you were in uniform. Because you were a good citizen doing your duty to support this policed state, people would pick you up and take you home.

In the canteen, we used to have this bench that had a till on it, and the men would come in one door, queue up, order their sweets and condensed milk or whatever, and go out the other door. We loved condensed milk in a can in the army because it was just instant sugar, which was great for energy.

One of the chaps I worked with was Purta, who always used to say he wasn't Afrikaans even though his name was Purta. He would refuse to speak Afrikaans to the Major's wife, who ran the stock room. Whenever he and I used to order stock from her, I would always try and speak Afrikaans, but he refused point-blank.

I have spent a great deal of my life judging myself, criticising my every thought, evaluating my every deed and feeling. And whilst developing the practice of mindfulness, I've been able to let go of the thoughts that do not serve me. Mindfulness has been a welcome and a curse for I know that I am so much more conscious of the thoughts that do not serve me. And I know that mindfulness is a lifetime practice. This doesn't sit well with someone who has a *hurry up* driver as well as a *be perfect* driver.

Growing up in South Africa, I found this critical evaluation of myself took hold of me not least of all when

I was being abused. Wanting to go back to my abuser. Caught in a trap of self-loathing and self-harm, fuelled by my absent father and his own critique and judgement of me. I was a hard-wired to be critical of self and other white South Africans. I could have done more to help others less fortunate than me. Why didn't I take up the struggle against apartheid? Why didn't I stand up and be counted? I could have stood up against it. I didn't.

Sometimes while we were serving, Purta and I would take it in turns to have a little snooze. The counter had a space underneath it, so we would lie under the counter and go to sleep in the middle of the day, fully clothed in our boots and everything. Whilst it wasn't hard work in the camp, the hiking and going home every night was quite tiring. Pretoria was at least forty-five to fifty minutes in the car from home, so it would take me about two and a half hours to get home, and then I'd have to go back every morning. So we used to lie under the counter and go to sleep. Taking a load off. It wasn't as if there was a huge amount of space either. There was only about fifty centimetres of space, so we were literally lying on a shelf. I was sleeping on a shelf under the counter.

Even though I hated it, I did have fun in the army too. I met this chap, Max, who was so outwardly gay, and I admired him. I thought he was fantastic. We used to go to gay bars in Pretoria, and I remember thinking to myself, *this is me*. The irony is, my wife-to-be didn't even notice, and Max used to come and stay with us.

The army was really weird for me. Not least of all walking into the showers and seeing all these fit men and thinking to myself, *I find you really attractive, but I'm not gay. I'm a fucking homophobe.*

My lesson from the army is that you shouldn't do something just because other people want you to. I supposed I lived that by trying to get out of it, which was my way of rebelling against the system. My tiny white privilege stand against apartheid. But it was also me taking a *yes...and* approach to my situation. How can I best survive this? I am not suggesting a *yes...and* approach solves all ills. It simply opens your mind up to the pool of choices available to you.

It's funny. It wasn't until recently that I let go the shame and guilt of being white South African. I made a conscious choice to let go. I was sitting at dinner with a group of CEOs and entrepreneurs, and the chat was normal dinner table chitchat. There was wine of course. We got onto politics, and South African politics came up. I am not entirely sure what possessed me, but I said, "*I feel such guilt and shame for the atrocities in South Africa. But more so about not having done anything. And my parents? Why didn't they do anything?*" I continued.

Now I wasn't hoping dinner would be my Truth and Reconciliation Commission, I was just sharing my story at the time. Then the most profoundly simple response came my way. So simple. So obvious. I had never given it the light of day. "*Deon, you need to forgive your parents.*" There was silence. I had a choice. My heart pounding in my chest. Outer clarity of mind. Everything seemed crystal-clear and noiseless. I could hear someone chewing on the other side of the restaurant about fifty feet away. "*Deon, you should forgive yourself.*" That was it. I had chosen shame and guilt, again. And that struck me hard. I chose an alternative that evening.

Try out having a *yes...and* attitude for a day. If that's too long, for an hour. Notice your ability to make conscious choices that serve you.

Perhaps at work in a meeting, agree that everyone present start each sentence with *yes...and*. Notice the positive contribution and creativity, but more importantly, people will feel they are making conscious choices that serve them and others.

Alternatively, play with a *yes...but* attitude and see what happens. So in an ideas session, get everyone to start their sentences with *yes...but*, and see how far you get.

My Vulnerability Gave Me Confidence to Share My Truth

I was working with a client just the other day in a one-to-one. I met him in a lovely café in the Surrey countryside. We always meet there; it's equidistant between our two businesses. There was a brilliant winter sunshine, and we ordered lunch and sat at a large country kitchen table in comfy armchairs. Ah, this is how to do business!

I was helping him get to grips with his purpose and then use that as a mission statement to live by. There I was, sitting there, eating, and Andrew turned around and said, "*How did you come upon your purpose and what's important to you?*" I found myself being quite open, more so than I would normally. I'm not saying I wouldn't be open, but I was quite vulnerable in a way, and that vulnerability brought about a deeper connection and understanding. And I know we all know that's how to do that, but it struck me in that moment. I can't control everything. Sometimes I must let go. Sometimes I just need to breathe, relax, and have faith that things will work out. Trust.

I'm very good at distracting myself, at deflecting. And that's what I was going to do with Andrew, but I stopped myself. It had such a powerful impact on him. We all need to be open to sharing parts of ourselves. How else can we live fully?

When Andrew asked that question, I thought, how much do I share here? What degree of self-disclosure should there be? What might happen to the dynamic of our relationship? Will sharing be useful for him? For me? Going with my gut, I began to talk to him about how I discovered my truth, my purpose, and put a plan together to speak it and live it.

A huge part of my discovery was going to places mentally and emotionally that were challenging. But I shared them all. My emotions are unbridled. I have never really had the gift of temperance. I never want to have perfunctory conversations anyway.

Andrew sat there listening. I was astounded by my openness and his keenness to hear my story. I'm not saying I hadn't been open with him, but it was the degree of openness that surprised me. Sharing my experience made me feel vulnerable. My vulnerability helped me connect with my stories and allowed us to connect on a deeper level, which can lead to a fuller understanding, and at work in business it can lead to increased collaboration, productivity, and cohesiveness.

What do you think about when you hear the word vulnerability? For many people, the term is linked to negativity, such as software weaknesses, personal mistakes, or professional danger. But embracing vulnerability is actually crucial to workplace success. I showed Andrew the vulnerable Deon, a side of me not many see.

We spent time creating a deeper connection that changed our relationship. Andrew and I understood each other better that day. In twenty minutes, our business relationship moved to another plain. This gave Andrew the confidence to share stories which we both agreed formed the backbone of his purpose.

My vulnerability gave me confidence to share my truth. When we share in this way, oxytocin is released in the brain. This feeds that feel-good feeling you get when you've done a good job, achieved a goal, or eaten chocolate. A deeper sense of trust is developed, and our relationships change.

Everyone has vulnerabilities, emotions, and personality components for good or bad. By hiding those vulnerabilities, we are essentially denying a major part of our personalities.

Being vulnerable means taking a risk, which can be daunting for one employee to do, but when all employees, and certainly leaders, feel comfortable taking the vulnerability plunge, everyone can benefit. Embracing vulnerability can look different for everyone. Start by noticing how you behave at work, who you are. Notice too who you are at home – are they the same person? Most probably not. Well not entirely. Most people let themselves relax and be comfortable at home, so try to embrace similar principles at work. See if you can bring to work a version of self you wouldn't ordinarily do. Notice the impact, for you and for others.

Next, use that personality for real conversations. People want to work with a human, not a robot, and most people are excited to talk about their personal lives and emotions, either good or bad. Build connections with co-workers through real, honest conversations. Having open, non-judgemental conversations fosters an environment of cohesiveness and teamwork where people feel they can share issues and ideas, both personal and professional, in a safe atmosphere. That emotion can also translate to the boardroom. Don't be afraid to get invested and show emotion about a project or report. You might not always be successful but getting emotionally invested in a project encourages others to do the same and can improve employees' morale and excitement.

Vulnerability is still somewhat of a taboo term in many workplaces. However, as more leaders and employees capitalise on their vulnerabilities, workplace environments can become more conducive to real connections, growth, and opportunities to increase trust, engagement, and respect, which are all important factors for success in the future of work.

Recently, I have helped a seemingly confident successful senior exec based in the US recognise his conscious choices and see what more he is. David runs a multi-million-dollar IT systems firm in San Fran. He is in his late forties, extremely fit and healthy, and never does anything by halves. A year before we met, he ran Marathon Des Sables, which is five marathons in five days in the Sahara Desert. David wanted more from himself. I helped him find the answers to *what more can I do?* Our work together had nothing to do with self-confidence. David oozed confidence out of every fibre of his being. People loved David.

On our all-inclusive, three-day retreat in the lovely Surrey countryside, David stopped acting and started performing. He began to fulfil a role. He came to realise a personified version of self he hadn't envisaged. Ever. The conversation went along like this:

"David, why do you feel you need to act? When I ask you to share a story from your past, you seem unconnected to

the events you are talking to us about. You appear to be showing us."

"I'm being me."

"Yes, you are, to an extent. But I don't believe you."

"What don't you believe?"

"You."

"What will you have me do then?"

"It isn't do, it is feel. I want you to get clear on how you felt in the moments you are describing and live that emotion here and now. With us."

"I can't do that. It's too intense. Inappropriate."

"It isn't for this residential. It may be for the boardroom. But try it here."

I asked him to focus his attention on his breathing and allow his feelings to appear. To be vulnerable. As long as you can still breathe a breath, you will be conscious of your feelings and be able to let them go. You will be able to choose feelings that serve you. That serve your intent. This will give you a clarity of mind, not an eagerness to finish. David let go of *what's next* thinking and began to feel with detachment. Master Luke Skywalker in *The Last Jedi* said to Rey, "*breathe. Reach out and feel.*"

The act of mindful breathing erased his compulsive and addictive patterns of talking at breakneck speed, of rushing forward to the next thought, and allowing what he had said to have impact. This had a profound influence on what his audience believed him to be as they watched. This simple exercise fundamentally altered his understanding of what more he could be.

Sometimes, the best thing I have done is not think, not wonder or imagine, and certainly not obsess, but just breathe and believe that everything will work out as it should. Perhaps not as I might have wanted it to.

This breathing exercise is to help you release nerves and tension, be present, and experience emotions without attachment. Allowing yourself to connect and be appropriately vulnerable. Integrating belly-breathing will, over time, have an impact on your state of mind, body, and well-being. You will become more present.

The Practice: Belly-Breathing

- Sit comfortably or stand in a neutral position – "centred".
- Starting from the top of your head, move your awareness slowly down through your body, noticing and releasing any tension.
- Lay one hand on your belly and one hand on your chest so you can notice where your breath is. When we sit or stand, our habit is to breathe up in the chest.
- If you have trouble feeling the breath in the belly, imagine you're breathing through a straw. Try inhaling through your nose.
- You can also experiment with filling your entire lung capacity, breathing into both the belly and the chest. Imagine your inhalation is like filling a glass with water, beginning from the bottom – the lowest part of the belly – and filling to the top – the top of the chest. Once you have taken this very big breath in, try letting it out in a big sigh of relief.
- Finally, return to your regular breathing, just noticing the rise and fall of the belly with your breath.

Everything works out in the end. You don't need to know how, just breathe and trust that it will. I didn't for so many years. The best way I have become a natural belly-breather is to undertake a daily practice. Since it's easiest to locate belly breathing when lying down, take two minutes before you go to sleep at night and when you wake up in the morning doing the exercise above. After a couple of weeks, you will notice yourself more naturally breathing this way as you go about your day.

I Must Stop Trying to Make it Happen and Just Let it Happen

I have never watched *RuPaul's Drag Race* – google it, if you don't know what I am talking about – but I want to find that version of self. David, my long-term partner of nearly nineteen years, and I used to go to this gay bar in Belfast called the Kremlin. We had a mutual friend Paul. He decided we should have drag names when we were out. It's a gay thing. Well, for some of us gays. I came up with the name Gina String. David was Suzi Summer, and Paul was Ronda Relish. We were just messing about. We'd talk and act out our names. Looking back, it was our way to perform. It was a way to be playful. A role to fulfil. Another version of self.

The oxford dictionary defines to *perform* as fulfilling a role. As an actor, when I am required to fulfil a role, I must bring certain emotions to bear. I must behave in a certain way. I must think in a particular fashion. I believe the same applies to everyone in life. Including leaders.

I help people come to terms with who they are and their purpose and how to use emotion to connect with people and how to do that in a public speaking context or any other leadership context. But what we're talking about really is disclosure, sharing some degree of one's self. Without doubt, just belief.

When Has Mr Doubt Consumed You?
When Have You Felt Just Not Good Enough?

Waking up one morning writing this, I was struck by how strong my sensor was. My inner critic. This is not right, Deon. This doesn't flow. My *be perfect* driver was kicking in. I didn't know what to say.

I find it peculiar that I'm writing and have written quite a bit for years in the form of blogs etc. I had such a block about writing at school. Mr Ford, my English teacher said once, "*You will never amount to much more than a D in your finals. That's a good target to aim for, Deon. It's achievable for you.*" I'm sure he meant well from his own point of view. Sure, he knew what I had produced thus far. He was making this judgement based on the work I had done. But fuck me, that has stayed with me ever since.

However, I don't always remember struggling to write. When I was about twelve, I sat at my desk in my bedroom, and I wrote this short story set in outer space. It was clearly inspired by *Star Wars*. It was set in outer space, but the characters wore Victorian costumes. The boy who was the hero got abducted I think. They all flew around in spaceships and had laser guns.

It was handwritten on paper, and I used carbon paper to make more copies. For each page, I had maybe ten sheets of paper with nine sheets of carbon paper in between it, and I would write my book out. I think I must've had ten or fifteen copies. They were crappy and grainy because my hand would rub across the page. I stapled it together on the side, and it just looked like a pile of shit.

I gave it round to friends and to my mother. My brother

just thought it was a load of crap, of course. He didn't even bother reading it. That was my first step into writing.

It's funny to think that I loved to write before I started high school, and then I hated English literature. I think the difference has everything to do with doubt and belief. I wrote my outer space short story without any doubt. I knew what I wanted to write, and I believed in my ability. In high school, I didn't believe I was a good writer, and I doubted everything I wrote. And the difference between those two is monumental.

What holds you back from your truth? What stops you being the real you? From finding your inner power and fulfilling the role you know you ought to?

When it comes to finding, speaking, and living our truth, there are many obstacles in our way, not least of all the ones inside us. This inner critic is your survival brain. It is the *flight* part of *fight or flight*. It is driven by fear. It is part of your brain that tells you you can't be the leader you know you are. The father you are. The mother. Sister. Brother.

I have struggled with finding my true purpose and being brave enough to live it. Looking back at my life thus far, as I often do, I've noticed a pattern of events and feelings resembling the activity on an ECG monitor. For every peak, there's been a valley. For every leap forward, there's been a stumble backward – sometimes just an inch, and other times, what seemed like miles.

I recognise and embrace this now, and this has brought me a tremendous amount of peace. I used to think that success and personal development required a steady, consistent ascent toward perfection. After all, my most powerful driver was be perfect.

When I have struggled with something I've struggled with before, I have felt I've failed. Last week I did a talk to a room full of CEOs about finding, speaking, and living their purpose. I was insanely nervous. I made a lot of mistakes, not least of all not introducing myself. I was filled with fear. But hold on a minute, Deon, you've found your truth. You are living it every day now. Aren't you *being* it up here now, with these people? I was, but I was trying to be perfect. Last week, I experienced a professional setback. I thought I'd done something wrong.

Finding and living my purpose does not mean always doing and feeling better than I did the day before. That's not growth, and when I believed it was, growth wasn't what I was seeking.

I was seeking permanently better. Perfection. In that moment last week, I noticed I wanted persistent happiness – a reprieve from difficult, overwhelming feelings, and a sense that every day of my life I was one inch closer to the ideal. We all know that life and, let's face it, leadership, is about the journey. But in the back of my head in that moment, I believed it would have no purpose if not for the destination, which made it hard to honestly be the real me. The authentic, playful, sometimes camp and outrageous me.

When I have my mind fixated on *getting there*, and I am deeply upset by any seeming break in momentum, I feel like a failure. Not good enough. Angry with myself. But I'm not *supposed* to feel angry – I'd been cultivating my truth for years. I'm living my purpose goddammit! I must stop trying to make it happen and just let it happen.

Then in the car on the way home, I realised I am me because I doubt. I recognised that personal development and growth – that life – isn't linear. That every day our struggles with who we are stretch us, helping us come to a better understanding of our true nature. And I live my purpose and grow when I do my best to learn from and move beyond my challenges instead of obsessing over them. In the car, I whacked up the music – Pink's Fuckin' Perfect was playing – and I sang at the top of my voice. Difficult roads often lead to beautiful destinations.

But writing helps. It gives us the space to understand our emotions. And last week, I was found out. My client Mark read me like an open book.

I was explaining to Mark that there is an emotional scale, and we have the power to determine how far along the scale we sit from moment to moment, and he interjected, *"You're being emotional."* There was a long pause. *"You've had a dark past."*

And he was right. I have had a dark past.

There was silence. I could hear a tumbleweed. I could hear the cars outside. People talking in the distance. I hadn't heard this background noise until now. Then came the tyrant of my inner-critic. How had he seen this? What had I said? What had I been doing? What was my body language telling him?

I paused, took a deep breath, and said, *"Yes. I have been writing a book, and the period of time I'm writing about is dark."*

Mark could see this in me, and I knew it was okay to allow this conversation. It led us naturally to work through the very point we had been discussing. Emotion is truth. Releasing emotion is helpful as it gives you space.

But there is a science bit. In a recent study, psychologists discovered brain scans on volunteers showed that putting feelings down on paper reduces activity in a part of the brain called the amygdala, which is responsible for controlling the intensity of our emotions. When people wrote about their feelings, medical scans showed that their brain activity matched that seen in volunteers who were consciously trying to control their emotions. Writing about their feelings gave the volunteers time to notice their emotions.

When we are able to notice, we can then make the right choices.

In my line of work, I have to be conscious of my emotions. Much like leaders need to when in business. It fascinates me, in my experience of working with thousands of CEOs, that there is a desire to want to rid themselves of emotion. To rid the moment, when they are speaking to an audience, of emotion. They see emotion as negative, something they are unable to control.

Writing helps you notice the situation and next time choose an appropriate level of emotion. Conscious-driven, appropriate emotion propelled into use by noticing, can be driven by keeping a diary, writing a blog, or any other form of writing coupled with being able to notice your breathing. Therefore, writing makes you happier.

The Practice: Writing

This practice, done regularly, will help you deal with the self-judgment that inhibits you. Your inner critic consists of the voices inside your head that constantly evaluate you. It can be enormously useful to confront your inner critic and get these voices out in the open.

Write a letter from your inner critic to yourself that includes all of the nasty, judgmental things it wants to say to you. Explore why and in what situations your inner critic thinks that you're not good enough or that you're a failure. Try to accurately capture the authentic tone as well as the content of your inner critic's voice.

Then write a response letter, appreciating the inner critic for its usefulness in your life, but also distinguishing which of its messages you choose to listen to, and which are no longer useful. End by finding a way to make peace with your inner critic, acknowledging your continuing, maturing relationship.

The way I make peace with my inner critic is to:

1. Get out and hit a tennis ball or do something physical.
2. Keep a diary of the positive things I do each day, including good thoughts and feelings.
3. Remind myself of my good attributes.
4. Remember life's a journey with setbacks.
5. Laugh with myself and sing out loud (out of tune is brilliant).
6. Share my joy with others and ask them to share theirs with me.

We are all Intention/Intuition & Gratitude Even if You are Not Conscious of It

Intention is the home in which you can live purposefully, daily. It's the only real way to the truth of leadership – to know yourself, trust yourself, and be yourself. We are all actors on the stage of life.

In 2003 when I decided to become a jobbing actor, I started living intentionally. Up until then my life was a constant stream of directionless nothingness. When you're an actor, people presume you're not being yourself because you're playing a part, but that was when I started living my truth. There's irony in that I had to be on stage playing a part in order to know myself. It was such a turning point.

I act every day. You do too. Acting is the reality of doing. And doing leads to being. For if you do intentionally, i.e. with purpose, you are being. Not doing for doing's sake. No autopilot here, baby. You've heard the line, a flower doesn't try to grow, it just grows. A bear doesn't try to be a bear. It is a bear.

There is a great, huge body of research that shows that the radical acceptance of all of our emotions – even the messy, difficult ones – is the cornerstone to resilience, thriving, and being happy. I call it emotional agility. But in my experience, it is more than just an acceptance of emotions. What is important is the words we use to describe our emotions. The things we tell ourselves. Our intentions. If I keep telling myself I am brilliant at my Federer backhand and keep at it, I will eventually *feel* brilliant at it. Equally, and generally more easily, if I tell myself (consistently) I am crap at writing, I will believe I am so. I won't want to write. I also know that accuracy matters. In my own research, I found that words are essential. In coaching for example, asking incisive questions at the right time with the right words is imperative. NLP call it clean language or clean questions.

But we often use quick and easy labels to describe our feelings. *I'm stressed* is the most common one I hear. But there's a world of difference between stress and disappointment or stress and that knowing dread of 'I'm about to do a presentation'. When we label our emotions accurately, we are more able to discern the precise cause of our feelings and what scientists call the readiness potential in our brain is activated, allowing us to take concrete steps. But not just any steps – the right steps for us

We are all intention, intuition, and gratitude, even if you are not conscious of it. There is a reason for everything you do. And you show up with a certain way of thinking and feeling, a certain attitude. You use your history, the factual part as well as the emotional decision-making part, to inform how you are at present and what you will be over the horizon. And therefore, each time you are 'doing', you are behaving in a certain way. You perform. You fulfil a role. You are acting.

I remember when I was standing on stage playing Bill Sykes in *Oliver Twist* at the first round of auditions. I remember the day as if it were yesterday. It was in the summer of 2003. June in fact. In West London in this room in this very old Victorian house where paint was peeling off the walls.

I walked into this very long room that had huge, long windows on my right. The sun was piercing through. The refraction of sunlight had made some of the people on the panel at the front of the room in front of the unlit, dank fireplace wear sunglasses. At first, I said to myself, *What the fuck?* I found it funny. I do laugh at silly things. I was nervous. Like most of us when we are nervous, we tend to say stuff, wishing sometimes we hadn't. "*You look like a scene from Reservoir Dogs.*" I giggled. The panel didn't. They just looked blankly at me from behind their sunglasses. It must have been an intimidation tactic.

It was a brilliant experience. I had had so many auditions by then. This one I really wanted. Not one single thought stopped me. Nothing. No doubt at all. Total belief in self. Confident, emotion-filled, intuitive, and present. Why? I had a clear intention. I knew how I wanted to be. Who I was. Why I was there. Why I was speaking. I knew my reason for *being* there.

At about half four in the afternoon, that beautiful London summer afternoon light still bright and piercing, the warm smell of summer in the air, someone from the panel spoke. "*Could the following people please stay? The rest of you, thank you very much for all your hard work today, we will be in touch.*" Belly breathing. I felt my heart in my throat. *Please don't ask me to say anything. I can't. I have a cricket-ball-sized lump in my throat.* My name was read out. *Fuuuuuuuuuuuuuuuuuuuuuck!* aka Bridget Jones. *They want to see more of me. This has got to be a good thing, right?* See? In an instant, we can let doubt creep in. And it does. Doubt is as binding as belief. It's stealth-like. Snake-like. A rodent squeezing its way through the tiniest of cracks in your confidence.

Four people were asked back that day. We had to play out the scene from *Oliver Twist* where Bill Sykes has a go at Nancy in Fagan's Den. I continued as Bill. I was totes channelling my hero Ollie Reed. Yes, I know that's from the musical, but he was the best, most menacing Sykes.

Once we had played out the scene, the director thanked us, and we went on our merry way, chitchatting as we walked down the stairs. We did the proverbial actor goodbye, a hug, kiss on both cheeks. And that's it. And breathe. My lungs filled with warm, summer-scented air. Sunglasses on, I danced my way back to the tube. I loved my life. This was it. This was what I was born to do. No inner critic. No censorship. Just living my truth.

I got the job and worked for the company for eighteen months playing Bill Sykes and other characters across Europe. Yes, it involved TIE, Theatre in Education, but I didn't care. And no, it wasn't Hollywood or the West End, but I felt good. I was living my truth.

Life changes, right? We move on. We make choices. Sometimes we say we don't make choices, but I believe we are always making choices. We are making choices even when we think we're not making a choice. That is a choice in and of itself. No seriously, I believe that. When we are present in the world, we are pure consciousness, we can make the right decisions for ourselves. This is the Holy Grail in life and most certainly the Holy Grail when it comes to finding, speaking, and living your purpose. When you are standing up there, wherever there is, in front of three thousand people, in your team meeting, in the boardroom, in the canteen at work, or the kitchen at home in front of your children, be present. When we are fully present, we make the right choices for ourselves. We are intentionally being, and that is the reality of acting, of life. We give ourselves space to mine our history for tales that will help us *sell the point*. I know you know this. But do you do it? Do you live it? I hadn't. I did that day. And I have a great deal since.

How Can We Learn to be More Real from People Who Lie Professionally?

Isn't acting all about stepping onto a set and pretending to be someone else by performing rehearsed actions and reciting words written by others? What could possibly be more untruthful?

Acting is the reality of doing. In my experience, actors play a variety of roles, so do we as leaders play many roles. How many roles do you play each day of your life? CEO, parent, spouse, engineer (or some other profession), citizen. Do you behave differently in each role? Yes, you do. Are you therefore not being real? You are *intentionally being* these roles. Beneath all these roles is the same person: you. The same is said for the actor.

Life is about doing. Not trying to do, just doing. And failing. And doing. And failing and doing. Which eventually leads to living intentionally. Even Yoda said it. "*Try not, do.*" Doing leads to being when you believe. Doing and believing are intertwined and are the primary things necessary for succeeding. And I think that's why when I was a jobbing actor, I thought I just had to go and do it. Believe. And be it.

I was a jobbing actor for a long time, and that was

when I came into my own. I recognised the value of living intentionally. Living with purpose. However, I still had to do something to earn money, so I applied for a job I saw to be a coach at Global Elite, coaching senior executives on how to present at an interview and construct a CV for themselves that was really powerful. Okay, I'd been in HR, and yes, I'd been responsible for recruitment, and I knew what a CV should look like, and I suppose I could stand up in front of a group of people, but I'd never been a coach before. Some call it *fake it to make it*, but I find that phrase quite difficult because being it comes back to believing. It might have seemed like I was faking it, but I believed I could do it, and I did. I don't see that as faking it. I was less capable and less competent at it to start with, but I wasn't faking it. I was *being* as much as I could in that moment.

Yet, all the while, I didn't think I was good enough, or I thought someone would find me out. I've always had this feeling that someone will find me out. I'm just little me. What do I know? But I kept on being.

I was going all over the place: Hamburg, Berlin, Paris, New York, and all over the UK. I helped these executives, these CEOs, be themselves and present better both in terms of what their CV said and in terms of how they came across in an interview. I helped them realise the essence of them. I helped them live intentionally. I just didn't call it that then.

I had no experience. No concept of what coaching a CEO was like or meant to be. Yeah, I had been a teacher, but not a coach. I just worked on pure intuition. Balls. But I did it. I helped them discover their story and use *appropriate, relevant* emotion in their stories to influence the interview panels. I taught them how to *act themselves*. And that helped me make money to pay my rent as an actor.

There was this Russian teacher of acting, Konstantin Stanislavsky. He taught that actors on stage should experience the emotions they were portraying. So, to portray a character's anger, for example, an actor should find real anger within him and express that in his performance. In short, he demanded that the emotion needed to be real in order to drive the action. The actor needed to know his history, his story. What was important to him or her – what he or she stood for – asking *who am I?* He or she needed to be clear about their purpose and in every moment, in every scene, needed to know what their intent was. The actors must ask themselves, *how do I want to show up?* As an actor myself, I have always been concerned with authenticity more than anything else.

So, to play something real on stage or film, an actor needs to express real emotion. Why do we spend most of our working lives devoid of emotion? Shying away from it. Unwilling to express who we truly are – the good with the bad.

It's a paradox of the theatre that *to pretend*, the actor must be real. He must show real emotion derived from his story. The actor must delve inside himself because the only way an emotion can be authentic is if it comes from within. In my humble opinion, the same principle applies to leadership. Over the years of working with thousands of executives, the one differentiating factor is the leader's ability to be emotional. Exposed. Vulnerable. Yes, emotion-full. Their ability to bring appropriate relevant emotion to bear. And to do this, they need to know who they are, why they are here, and how they want to show up.

There are so many layers of us, and there are so many versions of self. How do you know which is your true self? I think the only way you know your true self is to know your story, know the things that are important to you, and live by those things, those values. I didn't for a long time. I had very skewed values, fucked up values.

Letting the thoughts and feelings be, and not being driven by or consumed by them: that's the holy grail of a truthful performance on stage, on film, in leading, and for life. *You* must connect with your stories, allowing the emotion in your experience to come out. You must be able to use the emotion and feelings present in your story to connect with others. Bringing appropriate relevant emotion to bear moves you from doing into being. Letting *it* happen. I am not suggesting becoming an emotional wreck. Imagine you standing in front of your team blubbering whilst taking them through the dip in sales revenue. Hilaire. I am saying you must feel *it*. You should bring *appropriate, relevant* emotion to bear. But how?

Figuring Out What's Important to You and Using Stories to Connect is Action for Happiness

Walking up a mountain can take its toll on you. I know I am not Mosses, but I did have a Mosses moment up the mountain recently. Walking in the beautiful mountains in Chamonix, I had a little aha moment.

It's ridiculously hot up there (well, it can be cold too). The air is quite thin. It's very clean to the taste. I guess the air fuels a sense of reflection. Hence why I was up there in the first place. I went there with a group of colleagues on a retreat. It was a great time to think about what was important to me. I did this, as I have done over the years, by telling some of my colleagues about me. The whole experience was meant to be about walking up a mountain and talking. By the way, I am not suggesting getting to truly know what is important to you, you have to walk up a mountain, but it can help.

There I was walking up a mountain telling people from my tribe about a significant story of mine, marrying my ex-wife, Jeanette. All the while, I had difficulty with homosexuality. I associated homosexuality with my sexual abuse, so I became quite a homophobe, and yet I was this fabulous camp fucking queen. At college, I had an obsession with collecting keyrings, and I minced around college with my books and whatever and these keyrings. Mince, mince, mince. But I was such a homophobe.

When I was at university, I met Jeanette, who was this third year, and we became really good friends, and then we became lovers, and then I proposed to her when I was in the army, and then we got married because I wanted to do the right thing. That was another big thing for me: doing the right thing. Jeanette and I ran away and got married because her parents weren't going to say yes.

Jeanette's mother came to see her when she was in Pretoria. She agreed to meet us one afternoon on her way home, and Jeanette and I agreed that this was the time to tell her. I can still see her sitting in her car in some open-air parking lot in the driver's seat, and we just said, "*By the way, we're married.*" Boom! It was that kind of conversation. "*Oh right. Congratulations!*" Her face said it all. The grimace. The shock and anger were plain to see. She acted like it was great and she was happy about it. And I remember Jeanette saying, when her mother had driven away, that it was weird. She wasn't going to be that happy. And she wasn't. The next day she came back with Jeanette's father, and all hell broke loose. It was awful. They cut her off and never wanted to see her again.

We didn't get married in secret; we just didn't tell them. My mother was there. My father was there. My brother was there. None of her family were there. Why? It was a quick, let's-get-married-in-court type of affair. My father wasn't going to be there, but we realised I was only twenty, and that meant I had to have my father's consent to get married because you had to be twenty-one. It was all too forced. Unnatural.

We left, and I picked up the phone to call my father,

and I said, "*I'm getting married. Please come to the court because I need your consent.*" We drove to the court, and I got married. He didn't know I was getting married. I told him that morning. I was determined to do this, come hell or high water. Controlling what others think of me. Controlling what I think of me. Covering up for something.

After a while, Jeanette's parents started to come round to the idea. They lent us furniture, and then they fell out with us again. There was this unnatural control they wanted to have over people, over us. Much like mine. So they came by months later to come and collect the furniture again. To take it away from us. I was never good enough for their daughter anyway.

So they later came to collect their stuff, and they got some dude who was living on their farm to help them take it back. This guy decided to beat the shit out of me. I was arguing with Jeanette's father about something in the car park, and all the neighbours in the flats were coming out and checking what was going on, and then this guy just attacked me. And it was like something out of *Jeremy Kyle*. Jeanette jumped on his back and started hitting him, and he was fucking punching and kicking me. In front of all the neighbours.

That wasn't the first time I got beaten up. I got beaten up by three Afrikaans men in Pretoria because I was gay. I wasn't out though. I was with my friends Trudy and Dawn walking back to college, and they just decided to jump me and beat the shit out of me.

I got beaten up because I was gay, and then I was beaten up because I argued with my ex-wife's father. I was a lover not a fighter.

After Jeanette's parents had taken their stuff back, we had nothing. For about a year, my mother helped us financially as much as she could, and we set up in this really fucking dingy flat in Benoni. We didn't even have a cooker; we had a sort of two-plate stove. But it didn't matter because we were in love. Even though I was this raving queen. We had this amazing friendship, and I'd never been so connected to another person. We had a sexual relationship too, but it was never that great. Afterwards, I'd still feel like I wanted to go and have that shower like I did after the countless incidents of sexual abuse.

If you don't have a mountain to go to, bring the mountain to you. Start exploring your stories by completing your River of Life.

On one level, the purpose of this exercise is to find more stories and build a collection of stories to use to connect, engage, motivate, and influence others. This exercise also serves to help you reflect on your life experiences and discover moments where your experiences have influenced the things that are important to you. The exercise will also help you acknowledge you have stories to tell. It will help you recognize the significance of some of your stories, and in time, the exercise (if repeated) will help you begin to discover your why and your purpose. Exciting, I know!

Remember, to wholly live your truth, you must build a practice of self-reflection. Once you have completed your River of Life, use it as a reference guide for your stories. Go back over your river regularly. Reflect on your life experiences. Find other stories in your life that resonate. The stories don't have to be epic, they can be simple, everyday stories. Use them to connect with who you are and how you influence others. Using your stories will have meaning for you. You will bring appropriate relevant emotion to bear. You will have power and impact and an authenticity no-one can question.

Whilst at drama school, I started exploring the real me. I met this fella, Richard, in Chariots gay sauna. The bizarre thing is, we started seeing each other. In my eyes, you didn't see people after meeting them in a sauna. But hey, what did I know? That was the beginning of the end of my marriage. After I came back from drama school, I ended it with Jeanette. I went back and told her. We had bought a house together in the country, a lovely three-bedroom thing. We had a cat and a dog and all that. And then I told her, and it all blew up. She wanted Richard's number, and she called him and said, "*Do you know this is Deon's wife?*" It was like a scene from the movies. It was awful. She was screaming and crying, and so was I.

We screamed and cried and argued until five in the morning. Then the next morning, I said, "*Okay, I'm not gay.*" I didn't want to hurt her any more, and I said to myself that I'd live this lie for the rest of my life. I couldn't face my truth.

We sold the house and went on holiday to Ibiza because that's what married couples do. Not. We really sold the house because I knew what was coming. We really went to Ibiza because I wanted to go to Ibiza town. When we were walking around the street markets, I bought myself a rainbow purse. But I'm not gay. I'm not gay. I love cock, but I'm not gay. I didn't want to live the truth. I didn't want to face it.

We had a huge argument in Ibiza because she started

to notice things. She was slow to notice because she was in love. In love and in denial. We argued because I didn't want to have sex. "*If you want to go and have sex with a man, then go out and have fucking sex with a man!*"

After we sold our house, we rented this wretched two-bedroom house. I was still going through counselling, and I got into running a lot. I went for a run one evening in December 1998, and I went past my friend's house. She was a girl, of course. I didn't have any bloke friends. I went in for a cup of tea or something, and she looked at me and said, "*You need to tell Jeanette.*" She was right. So I ran back home, and that night, I told her I was gay and that I was leaving. It was time to call it a day. We did.

Jeanette was a very courageous woman. I don't think she realised it, but she was. She was a very giving person, which made it even worse.

We separated on the fourth of January 1999. That Christmas was shit. Really shit. And that was the end of my heterosexual life. Come to think of it, I didn't think my sexuality would be anything more than a choice about who I shared my bed with. But I was wrong. I had hidden away – buried underground – a version of self for so long I hadn't realised the significance coming out would have for me.

And then I fucking ran out of the closet. But this time, it wasn't in a public loo or a field or on a common or something. I went somewhere, and someone wanted to be with me, and I wanted to be with them. It was totally different.

Working recently with a CEO of a global corporate business, my brief was to help him get ready for a very important business-defining public speaking engagement. He was to be the keynote speaker at a global industry conference with over a thousand delegates. For Alan, this was a big deal. Alan was a good speaker. He had to be; he was a CEO. He had presented in business all his life, but something was missing for him. This wasn't about presenting. This wasn't about just sharing data. This was about him and who he was and what he represented. He needed to talk to the conference delegates, not present.

We spent four hours together. His first task was to complete the River of Life exercise before our initial meeting. He didn't. *"I didn't have time, and I wasn't sure why my personal stories would be relevant for this audience."*

I got him to stand up and present what he normally would. He shared some data and core messages. Factual. Very useful. But dull. I shared my thoughts – obviously in a constructive fashion using feed-forward – convincing him to explore the possibility that his stories could bring the data to life. He could be inspiring.

We began the exercise in earnest. Working through the exercise together, he noticed he had some deep and meaningful stories he could use as well as light, funny anecdotal stories which could bring the data to life. I asked him to take three moments in his life and to talk to me about them, relating them to at least one or two of the core messages within the data.

"I don't know how to do that!" came his reply.

"You think you don't." I sensed this was a time to be direct. *"Let go of the desire for it to be perfect. Have the intent to play and explore. Be curious about your stories and how they could relate to your core messages."*

Alan got up and started talking about his stories. Almost instantaneously, he had one of those aha moments. His stories gave him the freedom to relive and connect with who he was whilst speaking (not who he was from his past). He connected the stories to the messages. He made the stories relevant, and the dull data not so dull. His letting go of his attachment to what he should be like and should sound like enabled him to relive the stories using appropriate, relevant emotion to connect his core messages to his stories.

His intent (the way he was being), core messages, and stories fitted perfectly together. He was in that moment being a truthful leader. Alan invited some colleague into the room. "*Let's try this out on others, Deon.*"

Let's face it, we can never get away from our need for recognition. We are needy. Even the most confident of us need approval. The reaction Alan got was just what he needed. Alan received a more significant degree of approval when the thousand-strong conference room stood to their feet and applauded him and his keynote.

Your truth as a leader lies within you. Allow yourself the freedom to mine it and trust you will let it out relevantly and appropriately. Let it happen.

A tried and tested way to discover your stories is to complete The River of Life exercise. This exercise will help you build a collection of stories to use in any scenario. It can also help you reflect on your life experiences and discover moments where your experiences have shaped your core values. Once you have completed this exercise, I strongly suggest taking a brief note of the stories that resonate with you. Perhaps have a little black book. Note the stories, the core messages in them, then keep this book with you always, and whenever you are about your day and notice things and people, make a note. In other words, begin to create a bank of stories you can use.

The Practice: The River of Life

- Find a quiet space to work where you won't be interrupted for at least twenty minutes.
- Get a large sheet of paper and some coloured markers. You can spread out on the floor or tape your paper to the wall.
- Before you begin, take a moment to relax, breathe, and be present. Imagine that you are on a retreat and have all the time in the world.
- Draw a river on the piece of paper winding from the lower left corner to the upper right corner.
- Label the lower left *Birth* and the upper right *The Present*. Get creative! Break the rules!
- When you draw your river, let its shape and features represent what's special about your life. I've seen swamps, bridges, waterfalls, forked rivers, circular rivers. Don't strive for artistic perfection – improvise and surprise yourself.
- Cast your mind back over your life, and draw islands in the river, each representing places you've lived, key people you've known or who've influenced you, and any other 'landmarks' along the river of your life. Have fun with this – use different colours and symbols. Along each side of the river, add tributaries representing challenging and affirming moments from your life. Think of those events, decisions, choices,

79

and turning points that taught you something or made a lasting impact on who you are.

- Take a few minutes to look back over your river, adding any missing details. Make sure the river really captures every aspect of your life: family, work, spirituality, other life pursuits.

Once you've got this far, explore your river and note your insights:

1. What patterns or trends do you notice?
2. What experiences and people were especially significant?
3. What are the stories in your experiences?
4. What are the core messages in each experience/ story? Note these down in your journal.
5. How do you relate these stories to how your values have formed over time?

Here's some advanced river work:

Attach another piece of paper above the first and extend your river into the future. What do you envision happening in your own life, your family, your business? What key choices or decisions lie ahead? Where would you like to be in five or ten years? How can you use these stories in your talks and presentation?

Keep this river with you when constructing your next talk or presentation (take a photo of it on your phone). Remember, the key is about noticing your experiences. These experiences are rich stories you can use to connect with others.

Reflection Questions/Points:

1. What have some of your life stories taught you? What are the core messages in your stories?

2. Get a little notebook and write down words or phrases as reminders of your stories and the core messages within them. Keep this with you always. Add more stories and anecdotes as you go about living. Eventually you will build up a bank of relevant, usable personal stories.

3. Find moments to tell some of these stories to people. Even when not in a talk or presentation. Just in everyday life – at dinner, in the pub with friends. Notice how the story makes you feel when telling it. Notice people's reactions to you and your story. This can provide valuable insight into which stories to use and which parts of the story may not be necessary.

Body Language is a Powerful Dimension of Your Presence

When I walk into a room, I know, not in an arrogant way, that people notice me. People notice when there's an air of confidence and presence, but they also notice when it's the opposite. The latter is when I am not present. I am thinking about either the past, perhaps about something I may have done or said (totally unrelated to the present moment) or about some event or activity, allowing the thoughts and feelings to cloud the clarity of mind I can possess. I often hear myself tell clients, *depression or feeling down about something lives in the past, and anxiety lives in the future.* Alternately, calmness and peace of mind live in the present.

Recently, I went to a function for a friend of mine. It was their business's eightieth birthday. I walked into the room, and I didn't want to be there. People were turning around, noticing me not wanting to be there. I stood out like a sore thumb even though I wanted to dissolve into the crowd. I felt I was in a state of *lack*.

A different function, same day, different mind set, and certainly different intent. I notice my body language was playful, engaging, and open. I chatted. People noticed, they responded with similar interest. State of *flow*.

It's interesting that you can have such a profound effect

on a room, on a group of people, both from a positive and negative perspective. It's amazing the power we can have. It's also amazing the power one can have to be able to choose whether to walk in there head held high and wanting to engage with others, or walk in there and not, but still walk in there. There's a power in that choice.

The opposite of being at ease is seeking to control. When I was having sex for money, the exchange of money was part of being in control. £250 and I had six blokes fuck me. But there's a control and an inhuman condition that operates. There's almost an out-of-body experience. I was there but not present. It's the complete antithesis of the presence I'm talking about in here. It's not vulnerability because when you show a degree of vulnerability, there is a sense of humility in that; there's a sense of power in that humility. Getting paid for using my body was not being vulnerable at all; this was about being in control, making *them* think they were in control, but they weren't. And it was the same for that little boy who was raped, and that young sexually abused teenager.

Body language is a powerful dimension of your presence. The study and theory of body language has become popular in recent years because psychologists have been able to understand what we 'say' through our bodily gestures and facial expressions, revealing our underlying feelings and attitudes. Body language is one of the four dimensions of intelligence Tom Marshall talks about. He calls it the behavioural dimension.

Body language is the study of how people communicate face to face aside from the spoken words themselves. For me, body language includes facial expression, eye movement, and the physical movements of all parts of the visible body. I am not including breathing and perspiration – although these two are significant when it comes to perception and interpretation.

It's commonly and carelessly quoted that body language accounts for up to 93% of the meaning that people take from any human communication. This statistic is actually a distortion, and there is plenty of argument around whether you include communications with a strong emotional or 'feelings' element in this. I believe you have to be careful when stating specific figures relating to percentages of meaning conveyed or in making any firm claims in relation to body language and non-verbal communications. Suffice to say, what we do with our bodies when speaking to others has a huge impact on what they interpret.

In my experience, it is safe to say that body language represents a very significant proportion of meaning that is conveyed and interpreted between people. Many body language experts and sources seem to agree that between 50-80% of all human communications are non-verbal. So while body language statistics vary according to situation, it is generally accepted that non-verbal communications are very important in how we understand each other (or fail to), especially in face-to-face and one-to-one communications, and most definitely when it comes to speaking your truth, which obvs from now on involves an emotional element.

We form our opinions of someone we meet for the first time in just a few seconds, and this initial instinctual assessment is based far more on what we see and feel about the other person than on the words they speak. On many occasions, we form a strong view about a new person before they speak a single word. The effect happens both ways – to and from.

When we meet someone for the first time, their body language, on conscious and unconscious levels, largely determines our initial impression of them. In turn, when someone meets us for the first time, they form their initial impression of us largely from our body language and non-verbal signals.

And this two-way effect of body language continues throughout communications and relationships. Body language is constantly being exchanged and interpreted between people, even though much of the time this is happening on an unconscious level.

Remember, while you are interpreting (consciously or unconsciously) the body language of other people, so other people are constantly interpreting yours.

The Practice: Intent and Body Language

Next time you have a meeting, before the meeting, decide on an intent, how you want to show up. Pick a word that motivates you to behave in a certain way. For example, I might choose *thought-provoking*. When I am being *thought-provoking*, I do certain things with my body. My non-verbals are affected. We all do this. We are not the same situation to situation. Obviously, you must still participate in the meeting, but in this exercise, pay attention to your body. Notice what you choose to do with your hands, arms, eyes, your position in the room etc. when you have a *motivating* intention front of mind.

Reflection questions:

1. What did you notice about your body language? Was it any different?
2. What did you notice about how you felt?
3. Describe how you conducted yourself in the meeting. Identify just three words.
4. What did you notice about others' reactions to you?

Remember to feed-forward:

Ask yourself…

1. What did I do well when engaging others in the meeting I should do more of?
2. What could I do to improve next time?
3. What am I grateful for in myself?

The people with the most conscious awareness of and capabilities to read body language tend to have an advantage over those whose appreciation is limited largely to the unconscious. You will shift your own awareness of body language from the unconscious into the conscious by learning about the subject, and then by practicing your reading of non-verbal communications in your dealings with others. And this is why I always advocate never assessing the effectiveness of your speaking, or whether or not you connected with your audience, by reading into the non-verbal body language of your audience. You leave yourself open to misinterpretation. Instead, feed-forward on yourself, always. It breeds confidence and greater self-awareness.

I have noticed over the years a mastery of this thing I call presence – projecting a sense of ease. Well, perhaps not entire mastery, but certainly an ability to live it. An awareness of the emotional responses you have to your own thoughts and feelings as well as consciousness of external stimuli and your emotional responses to them, is a state of mind. When there is a clarity of mind – not an absence of emotion, the latter I believe is unnatural – you are able to connect authentically with the thoughts and feelings of others in the room. You are present. You tap into the limbic part of the brain, the part of the brain that controls emotional intelligence – our emotional ability to respond to stimuli.

I was a keynote speaker at a recent business event for about a hundred and fifty entrepreneurs. I was talking about this very thing – presence and its value for business owners. An audience member shouted out a question, some may say a heckler. *"You're being emotional!"*

"Yes, I am," came my reply. At this point, I was telling them a story about my experience of sexual abuse to highlight a moment of fight or flight. The story is in here in more detail. *"And how do you feel right now, sir?"*

He went on, *"Well, umm…what I mean is, you seem to be* overly *emotional."* I paused, giving myself space to experience my emotion, and then said, *"And how do you feel right now, sir?"* The man started shuffling in his chair. *"I don't know. I feel uncomfortable."* Another pause, *"Good."* I then turned to the wider audience and said, *"This is precisely what I mean when I say connecting authentically with the thoughts and feelings of others."*

Someone had an emotional response to what I was saying (and I know others had too). I went on to clarify that I was not suggesting to use stories of sexual abuse in business to facilitate a connection between you and your audience. What I was saying was that we human beings are emotional. When we use appropriate stories to convey a message, stories we ourselves connect with on an emotional level, others connect with us too. We tap into the limbic part of the brain which is the basis for all emotional response.

Whether you walk in head held high or not wanting to be noticed is all about flow. It's positive energy versus negative energy. For me, it's very much like playing tennis. When I'm in a state of *lack*, I'm concerned with how I need to move my feet, where the ball's going to go, who the opponent is, whether they're better than me, and I fuck it up. But when I'm in *flow*, when I'm not concerning myself with those things, I'm phenomenal at tennis. Well maybe phenomenal in my eyes. Perception is nine-tenths of the law.

It's exactly the same with improv. When you're concerned with the outcome, it falls to pieces. When I was directing *Your Line or Mine?*, I kept on saying to the actors, "*Stop playing for the laugh. Just play the truth in the story, and the laugh will come.*" I was told that once by Keith Johnstone, the improv guru, and he's so right.

When you're in flow and you're not concerned with the outcome or attached to an outcome, things happen. You have a presence. I believe life is about experiencing, just being, rather than having a set path and sticking to it. This allows you to experience the experience. When you're not in flow, and you're concerned about the outcome, you don't see or experience. You still have a presence. It just doesn't serve you or others.

Most people think you are born with presence or without it, or that circumstances lead you, if you're lucky, to develop it at an early age. And if the right circumstances never quite align, well, too bad. Fortunately, that's not the case. In my experience, presence is the result of certain ongoing choices you make and actions you take or fail to take. Presence is a set of skills some of which are driven by "the heart" (the limbic and initial layers of the neocortex parts of the brain), and other skills are driven by "the head" (the substantive neocortex – this is the seat of thought, containing the centres that put together and comprehend what the senses perceive). I believe that virtually anyone can develop and improve their ability to tap into these parts of the brain consciously, and then eventually subconsciously without the need for thought. That's presence.

However, when I say anyone can improve his or her presence, I don't mean it's an easy task. It may require you to give up habitual patterns of behaviour that you maintain because they make you feel safe. Developing presence will require you to go places and do things that feel uncomfortable, at least initially.

As leaders (of self and others), we ought not be solely focusing on making a better impression. Yes, being impressive is part of it. But to be truthfully impressive, we need to embrace presence entirely. We need to be truthful leaders.

Again, I am drawn to the theatre analogy. That's my life. Just because you have won the lead in a play or a leadership title at work doesn't mean you automatically hold any more sway over your audience or your team. It is your *performance* in both the theatrical sense and the organisational sense that will grant you the authority the title or role implies. In this regard, your *performance* is purely about building trust. To build trust requires you to have presence, be truthful, and bring real, relevant, appropriate emotion to bear. Living and leading intentionally, with purpose, in each moment. The truth (the presence) you bring to your role – how you show up, how you connect, how you feel, how you speak, listen, act – every move you make on the corporate or real stage, combine to create the impact you have.

Presence comes from within. It is released when you live your purpose, and it brings about an impact. It begins with an inner state. And how we deal with our inner world drives everything. Every aspect of how we love, how we live, how we parent, and how we lead. Our inner state leads to a series of external behaviours: the use of your voice, body language, eye contact etc. You can put on the behaviours, but by themselves they'll lack something essential. They'll be hollow noises and nothing else. Think about it. The conventional view of emotions as good or bad, positive or negative, is rigid. And rigidity in the face of complexity breaks you down. We need greater levels of emotional agility for true resilience.

In the political leaders debates of recent times, we've all heard politicians say, "*I feel your pain*," when we know they're simply saying what they think we want to hear. Now compare that to Martin Luther King Jr.'s *I have a dream* speech. His emotion came from his deeply held beliefs, and it motivated a generation to overturn four hundred years of assumptions and behaviours. Oh, and by the way, he never showed people a series of PowerPoint slides either.

A Lot of the Time We Walk Around Without Intention, On Autopilot

In South Africa, *sawubona* is the Zulu word for *hello*. There's a beautiful and powerful intention behind the word because *sawubona* literally translated means, *I see you, and by seeing you, I bring you into being.* So beautiful. Imagine being greeted like that. Imagine living like that. Leading others like that. But what does it take to truly see ourselves, our thoughts, our emotions, and our stories, all of which help us to thrive in an increasingly complex and fraught world?

After my *Oliver Twist* audition, I spent a few days agonising over whether I got the part. Oh, the doubt never goes away. So I called up the director with the intention to ask for constructive feedback. I genuinely wanted feedback because there was no way I'd got the job. But he said, *"What do you mean feedback on your performance? You were great. We want to offer you the job."* It was the best thing ever. It was the change for me. I started to believe in myself, and I started to say to myself, *Not I cannot, but I can.*

I spent eighteen months with that theatre company touring around Europe. I came back to London in the latter part of 2004. After that, I got a job in an improv troupe. Improv is about doing. Improv is about two core skills, *listening* and *responding*. There is nothing in improv about the outcome. In fact, holding onto an outcome destroys the scene. It is very much intent driven present-moment-ness.

The dictionary defines intent as intention or purpose. The adjective is defined as determined to do (something). A synonym for intent is attitude. And I define attitude as a settled way of thinking and feeling. I see intent meaning on purpose, planned, conceived. It's not accidental. It's not *I'll just see*. No, it's more like *I will*. Like sawubona. I see you.

Dr Wayne Dryer says, *"Our intention creates our reality."* By being purposeful about what we create and accomplish, we create our very reality. The intentions we set today influence the life we live tomorrow. The intent you set for your board meeting (when preparing) impacts the meeting you have. Think about intent, from a biological perspective. Every time we have an intention to walk or lift our arms, our intention incites millions of chemical reactions and electrical impulses that obey the laws of nature. Inherent in your desire is the mechanics for its fulfilment. These mechanics apply intent far beyond the physical body. Intent is a clarity of mind: how we think affects how we feel and what we do.

I was watching my six-year-old son playing the other day. He was playing dress-up. He was a pirate. He asked me to join in. I instantly suggested we need a ship, some maps, and pirate clothes. And we needed to know who was who in our little pecking order. William turned and said, *"Dad, just play."* I was overcomplicating things. Packing in too much. Less is more apparently. I think we do this with leadership, with life. We pack in too much.

In the case of Dad and William playing pirates, the requirement was to have the intention to play. He wanted to trust me to just play with him. I wasn't playing intentionally. I was playing as I thought I needed to play. My excuse: I'm an adult, and I sometimes forget the best bit in this life is to be fully intentional. A child has this natural ability to be purposeful. It's the only way they know how to be.

Think of intent from a business perspective. You have a clear vision and mission (purpose/intent/aim/goal), and this is why you are in business. It drives everything you and your team do. It incites people in the business to behave in certain ways. It affects the way in which you do business, the way you and the team talk to clients, the way you engage with your market place. The mechanics of the business is driven by the intent of the business. A lot of the time we walk around without intention, on autopilot. I lived autopilot for years. Sometimes we run our businesses like this, burying our heads in the sand. We haven't formally articulated (to ourselves) what we desire to conceive for our talk, one-to-one meeting, or sales presentation, day, our week, or even our life. You know the saying, *fail to plan and plan to fail.* It's important to know what your intentions are so that you can move in that direction. So you can be your truth. There are many ways to set your intentions. Some people do it daily. Some people do it on a weekly basis. Some people combine intention setting with meditation. Some people just decide what they intend to do, be, or have.

I believe in focusing on what you want to do, be, have, feel, or create and working backwards to set an intention for your talk or meeting to align with those desires.

Intentions to me are a way of being that create a desired present and future. An important thing to note – intent is not a goal. You're not intending to lose weight. However, you might intend to be healthy and to make healthy choices. Your intent must be actions (to be productive), feelings (to feel love), and thoughts (to be optimistic). It is how you want to be. Your intent must guide your interactions with other people. Your intent affects how you show up. The question to ask yourself is *how do I want to show up?* Like the actor, you must have an intent for each interaction. Every scene of your life. And in each interaction, you are not going to be the same. Notice which intentions work well and which need not be used.

I was talking to a huge auditorium full of business owners recently. My brief was to help them be more confident with presenting their story. This last sentence was my brief, not my intent. My intention was to be inspiring and thought-provoking. This had real meaning for me. These two words (albeit that one was hyphenated) affected my mechanics. They were emotive for me. They were my vision and mission. They were my reason for speaking. *My why.*

I told them a few stories about me, then I unpicked each story, showing them what core elements are and how to craft a good talk. Then I got them to craft a sixty-second pitch/talk using personal stories with the person next to them. Intent is all about you. It must be motivational, memorable, and mine (yours). In other words, your mechanics need to be fired up by your intent. This is the piece of speaking that people never give time to. It is the most important aspect of speaking. It is crucial for leadership. Think of intent as how you are determined to be. Your desire for yourself. How you want to show up.

There I was in this improv troupe creating ninety-minute shows from nothing. With a framework, an intent, but with no fixed outcome or result. The shows would start with seven of us standing in a line in front of an audience with a clock behind the audience so we could tell how long it'd been and how long we had left, and the audience had to decide the order in which the actors came on stage. We would ask the audience to give us a word or single sentence or a person's name or a description of a place. We would then create a ninety-minute show by listening and responding to each other.

Connecting with each other was really important, but some people find it really difficult to make that connection because they may be unwilling to just be. This one fella, John, used to say, "*I don't have any problem doing any kind of scene. I don't have a problem with any kind of boundaries, so let's just go for it.*" Every time he tried to do anything in improvisation, it would either go down the road of sexual abuse or self-harm. It was always a light contribution to any kind of play. Even if we were creating a play about a happy family holiday, there was sexual abuse in it. He said, "*I have no boundaries, but none of the boys get to kiss me. Guys, please, I don't want you to touch me at all.*" Show a degree of vulnerability.

Any time John came on stage, we would suggest (and it was usually myself and my friend Annalea) out loud that Emma was John's sister or something. It would always end up with Emma having this relationship with John on stage. We'd do it for a laugh. It's funny now. In those moments, we were not really listening and responding, we were directing how it should be.

If at any point there's doubt when two actors are

interacting, in other words a point where there isn't clear intention, people see it as fake, as ham acting. The audience doesn't believe any more. And the scene falls apart. If at any point you question how you've thought, how you've been, how you said something, it shows up. Your audience will notice. Intent is a clarity of mind that produces certain behaviours. It's an interesting metaphor that works for business too.

Doubt is as binding as confidence, and I totally and utterly have experienced that and get it. I think that's why I'm so reluctant at times. I'm reluctant because Mr Doubt has crept in. Doubt makes me wonder if I'm doing the right thing. And I think the same thing applies to business. The main thing people I work with doubt is whether they are good enough. Good enough for now, good enough to create even more success. I help them focus on *being* rather than thinking about what the outcome should be. Over time, doubt gets diluted and confidence ensues. As soon as you focus on the outcome, doubt creeps in. Focus on you and your intention and your purpose, be sure of your call to action for the audience but be unattached to it. Watch how in flow you will be.

Every Aspect of Leadership is Potentially a Speaking Opportunity, and it is Ripe for Preparation

Let's consider some practical applications of intent-driven leadership. Consider you as a speaker. You are, right? That's what you do as a leader: speak, engage, communicate, compel, motivate, inspire etc.

For every interaction and scenario (i.e. for life):

1. Get clear (for yourself) on how you want to show up.
2. Know what you want your listeners to think, feel, or do. Your call to action. Understand the outcome you want, and then let it happen. Detachment.
3. You've got to know what you're talking about – your core messages. Be clear (for yourself) of the nuggets you want your audience to take away.
4. What stories will you use to convey your core messages?

Let's have a play with the power of intent. I want you to understand the impact memorable, motivational, and 'my own' (mine) intent can have on any speaking-driven scenario. Use the passage below to practice this technique of owning your intent and never forgetting it whilst speaking. This is a playful exercise but has huge value when considering its application to your own communication scenarios. Remember, intent is not your call to action. It is how you want to show up.

The Practice: Intent and Voice

Find a private space and read through this paragraph out loud:

Mr Chops the butcher
Shuts his shop-shutter;
Or perhaps his assistant
Shuts his shop-shutter.
The butcher's shop-shutter
Is a short shop-shutter,
And the butcher's short shop-shutter
Should shut sharply.

Now read it again with the intent to read it to a group of four-year-old children. Imagine they are in front of you. Be sure to remember how best to read to a group of small children. Focus on what is important to *you* (how you want to show up) when reading to four-year-old children. Now read the passage again.

What did you notice was different from the first time you read the passage out loud?

Simply put, your intention drove the changes in pace, vocal variety, emotion, and energy. Intent has the power to alter what people understand from you. How you show up has the ability to affect the degree to which you connect to and engage an audience.

A further exercise to try is to find a poem you really like and then choose an intent. Forget about the audience for now. See how the poem changes from intent to intent. For example, you could choose to say it clearly and precisely. Then choose to say it playfully. Then review the differences between the two versions. Neither version is wrong. They are just different.

With an intent constituted by the three Ms (memorable, motivational, mine), you will always be sure of your mission when speaking, talking to others, leading the board meeting, or talking to your loved ones, and you'll certainly be the one people remember.

Once you notice your ability to use an intent to drive how you are and how you say things, use this self-awareness to cultivate real presence and trust with everyone you speak to. Go and try it out with some of the stories you discovered in your River of Life. Try telling the same story with a different intent. Notice the impact on yourself, on the words you choose, the emotion you bring to bear, the part of the story you tell, and the impact this all has on your audience. See if you can pick up from your audience their differing take-aways. Each time you have a different intent, the call to action will alter.

Some keys points to help you be intentional:

1. Know your values. Your values should always be a guiding light to your day. Any intention you have that doesn't align with your values is probably the wrong intention.
2. Know your vision, your leadership purpose. Make sure your intentions lead you to your vision. After all, your intention creates your reality.
3. Identify the activities, thoughts, and/or feelings that align with your intention.
4. Remind yourself of your intention. Make sure you don't lose sight of your intention. It may help to jot it down on something you can carry with you such as an index card. Ask yourself throughout the day or week, *Is this in alignment with my intentions?* If the answer is no, redirect your thoughts, feelings, or actions.

Reflection Questions/Points:

1. What did you notice was different in your vocal tone and pace – the way you delivered the tongue twister?
2. When in a speaking scenario, have a clear intent that is memorable, motivational, mine. Use feed-forward to review your success in using the power of intent.
3. Where might you use some of this new-found awareness of the power of intent to your advantage

when speaking?

4. Ask yourself these questions after every talk, presentation, or speaking scenario and use feed-forward to guide your responses.

Ursula, a senior executive in a global corporate financial services organisation, is asked to speak regularly to thousands of professionals across the globe. She's been doing it for fifteen years. She is formidable, a consummate speaker and leader who really knows how to engage an audience. Until recently, Ursula hadn't realised the power of intent, the effect a settled way of thinking and feeling could have on how she talked to her audiences. She would deliver her talks in much the same way she always had. She always got great feedback. Why wouldn't she? She was an exceptional speaker. Helping her use intent to drive everything she thought, felt, said, and did kept her speaking alive, energised, and on track, and made her audience understand her message more clearly.

"*I see an intent for my talk much like a vision and mission for a business. It's the driving-force behind everything. But I know I need to focus on the here and now. I feel different. People see me differently.*"

Even Marcus Aurelius way back when he was Emperor of Rome said, your intent has the power to alter other's perception of you.

The Practice: How Do I Want to Show Up?

Next time you are about to go into a meeting or have a conversation with someone, take about five minutes of your time – maybe go to the loo – and reflect on two questions. One, ask yourself, *how do I want to show up?* Identify one word that motivates you to walk into that interaction with a certain frame of mind and drives the *what* and *how* you say things, and how you act (your body language). The second question relates to your call to action. *What do I want them to think, feel, or do?*

For example, last week I was hosting a business networking dinner. My intent was to be curious. This motivated me to ask more incisive questions and listen more purposefully. My call to action was that I wanted the people I spoke to to feel like they were truly listened to. I wanted them to feel as though I cared.

Try it out. Give it a go. It's common sense. We do it unconsciously. I recommend you do it more consciously and notice the changes it has on you and on others you communicate with.

Remember to feed-forward:

Ask yourself...

1. What did I do well when engaging others that I should do more of?
2. What could I do to improve next time?
3. What am I grateful for in myself?

Let Your Body Do the Talking!

Body language is more than body positions and movements. It is not just about how we hold and move our bodies. Body language potentially (although not always, depending on the definition you choose to apply) encompasses:

- how we position our bodies
- our closeness to and the space between us and other people (proxemics)
- our facial expressions
- how our eyes move and focus
- how we touch ourselves and others
- how our bodies connect with other non-bodily things: pens, spectacles, and clothing
- our breathing and other less noticeable physical effects: heartbeat and perspiration

Body language tends not to include the pace, pitch, intonation, volume, variation, pauses etc. of our voice.

Arguably, this last point should be encompassed by body language because a lot happens here that can easily be missed if we consider merely the spoken word and the traditional narrow definition of body language or non-verbal communications. Voice type and other audible signals are typically not included in body language because they are audible, 'verbal' signals rather than physical, visual ones. Nevertheless, the way the voice is used is a very significant (usually unconscious) aspect of communication, aside from the bare words themselves. Consequently, voice type is always important to consider alongside the usual body language factors. Similarly, breathing and heartbeat are typically excluded from many general descriptions of body language but are certainly part of the range of non-verbal bodily actions and signals which contribute to body language in its fullest sense.

More obviously, our *eyes* are a vital aspect of our body language. Our reactions to other people's eyes – movement, focus, expression etc. – and their reactions to our eyes contribute greatly to mutual assessment and understanding, consciously and unconsciously. With no words at all, massive feeling can be conveyed in a single glance. The metaphor which describes the eyes of two lovers meeting across a crowded room is not only found in old romantic movies. It's based on scientific fact – the strong powers of non-verbal communications.

These effects – and similar powerful examples – have existed in real human experience and behaviour for thousands of years. The human body and our instinctive reactions have evolved to an amazingly clever degree, which many of us ignore or take for granted, and which we can all learn how to recognize more clearly if we pay attention. Our interpretation of body language, notably eyes and facial expressions, is instinctive, and with a little thought and knowledge, we can significantly increase our conscious awareness of these signals: both the signals we transmit, and the signals in others we observe. Doing so gives us a significant advantage in life – professionally and personally – in our dealings with others. Body language is not just reading the signals in other people. Let *your* body do the talking.

Importantly, Understanding Body Language Enables Better Self-Awareness and Self-Control

Body language helps us to understand more about other people's feelings and meanings, and we also understand more about these things in ourselves. When we understand body language, we become better able to refine and improve what our body says about us, which generates a positive improvement in the way we feel, the way we perform, and what we achieve. In the meantime, become a connoisseur of body language. Conduct these drills and integrate them into your way of being. Study others and observe self. Start with this simple practice. Note down your observations. Remember, non-judgement – detachment.

The Practice: Body Language

Become Aware. Next time you're in a public place, like a shopping mall or some large event, watch how people move. See if you can tell anything about them – their mood, physical condition, and personality – by the way they walk and hold themselves. When you meet a friend or loved one and have a chance to see them move, try to guess their frame of mind before they say a word.

Posture. People with presence tend to hold themselves

erect. If you slouch and let your shoulders round in, it could communicate a lack of confidence. However, correcting bad posture may take considerable effort. I often recommend Pilates training to get your body strong so it can release your shoulders and help you stand up straighter. Tai chi, martial arts, Alexander Technique, or yoga can help too.

Facial Expression. Some people prefer a poker face, one that reveals nothing about their state of mind. While we recognise there are some situations when a poker face might be useful, in general you will connect with others better if you allow your face to reveal what you feel. Not your nerves though. But your feelings you want to convey in the story you are telling. Think emotional-intent.

Mirroring. Subtly copy the other person's body language. Best done in one-to-one scenarios. Just as you can mirror someone else's voice, you can mirror their facial expressions. Facial mirroring says, *I understand you.* There's nothing more supportive than to look out at an audience and see facial expressions that say, *we're with you.*

Gesture. Notice how others use their arms and hands when they talk. Some people, some entire cultures, favour great expression. Others prefer to be more self-contained. There are appropriate times for both approaches, but in general, you'll communicate better if you use gestures that are congruent with what you're saying.

Eye Contact. Eye contact when you're expressing yourself is critical. Without maintaining eye contact, you risk losing the attention of the listeners. It's just as important in a meeting or presentation as in a one-on-one. In my experience, leaders and truth-speakers make two major errors. First, they want to include everyone, and so their eyes shift much too rapidly around the room. Or even worse, they speak to the back of the room. Second, they focus too much on looking at the materials they're presenting, whether it's a speech in front of them or a slide projected on a screen. In both cases, they haven't used their eyes to connect with the audience. Look at the audience. Look individuals in the eye. The people around them will feel you are connecting with them too. Don't stare though. Don't focus on one person alone for your whole talk/presentation.

Movement. This applies in particular when you're standing and speaking to a group:

Use the Space. Walking, especially in combination with pausing, can be a powerful combination. Make an important point, then pause, and while pausing, move to a different position. Then begin speaking again. (It's usually not a good idea to talk while moving.) If you're telling a story, let the different locations on your 'stage' represent different locations in the story (e.g. home and office) and move to those locations when the story changes scenes.

Remember though, any of this movement must be driven by your intent and not just implemented for movement's sake. If you do it for the latter reason, you will find you end up 'speaking by numbers'. Inauthentic baby!

Distance. Moving can change the energy level in the room. If you stand far from the audience – at the podium, for example – that's a safe, low energy place for you in relation to the audience. But if you move toward the audience, you create a more intimate connection. And, if it's physically possible, moving right up to or into the audience will pick up the energy level in the room enormously. Wake-up call. Whenever you enter some-one else's space – an individual's' or an audience's – you create a moment of high potential, even danger. Will you call on someone? What do you want? What are you going to do? People wake up when the speaker approaches. Be aware of that dynamic and use it to add energy and emphasis to your message.

Taking up space. Some people seem to take up more space in a room than their physical size alone would justify. These exercises will give increased confidence to your bearing:

- **Grounding.** Walk around in an empty room. See yourself as solidly grounded with your centre of gravity not in your chest but in your pelvis where your legs and hips connect. See yourself as solidly connected to the earth.

- **Expanding.** Then, see yourself as literally taking up more physical space than your body actually requires. Imagine you're much larger than you really are. Walk through the room with your arms extended wide. Imagine you're a king or queen, someone of enormous authority, because people usually give such figures a lot of space. Imagine you are in your own home, greeting and welcoming the people around you.

- **Owning.** Go into the room where you'll speak and make yourself comfortable with it beforehand. Don't be shy – this technique really works! If you can't get into the room, visualise it.

Try these different techniques and use feed-forward to reflect on their appropriateness. Remember, I am not asking you to critique yourself.

It's about practice. Try it and then feed-forward. Remember, it may feel clunky to begin with, but over time you will move from a conscious competence to an unconscious competence. Enjoy playing around with it all.

Remember to feed-forward:

Ask yourself...

1. What did I do well when engaging others that I should do more of?
2. What could I do to improve next time?
3. What am I grateful for in myself?

Charisma Itself is Not Necessarily the Villain, but Narcissistic Charisma is

When I was away in South Africa recently, I was getting attached. I kept thinking, *oh shit. I'm away for two weeks. What about income?* And I ended up texting Emma asking if she wanted to follow up on this chap I was trying to sign up. She told me to get a grip and let it go. She told me to stop being so attached. Everything was fine.

We all latch onto this attached-ness sometimes. It's driven by fear, of course. The fear of not being good enough, of not belonging, of being found out. All those rubbish things. But I believe in experiencing all the emotions, not just the positive ones. Remember to practice detachment when it comes to body language by letting go of your perception of what your audience might be interpreting and focusing on your intent. Stop the autopilot. Pay attention to your body and how to communicate the messages you are delivering. Presence varies with each individual.

As I have developed my work, the notion of charisma has fallen into disfavour. People call it fake news. Social media is riddled with it. Too many companies in recent years have come to wrack and ruin led by so-called charismatic leaders who have led their companies over the edge of the cliff while making barrels of money for themselves in the process. Think 2008 RBS crash.

Charisma itself is not necessarily the villain, but narcissistic charisma is. That's the kind of charisma that allows an individual to sway the masses and stir up followers while maintaining emotional distance or even disdain for those followers. I can think of a very famous campaign that led to the appointment of a leader of the free world where he most certainly possessed a disregard for the very people who put him there. But charisma as an element of true presence can be a tool for good, as long as the other elements are also in place. There must be a congruency between the inner state of mind and the external behaviours. How?

Heard a leader or speaker and known when he/she doesn't mean it? Of course you have. Have *you* ever not meant it but just said it anyway? This inner state is driven by the leader's intent. You know when the intent – their inner state, their heart and mind – is dishonourable. We've all seen it in recent days in politics. You witness the external behaviours of their voice and body language and use of the space. On the surface, they are charismatic. Meanwhile, back at the ranch, they are at best fibbing, and at worst deceitful, manipulative, and lying.

What's the Relevance for You?

The meshing together of the inner state (your intent) and the external behaviours is key. A presence-full state of being comes from using your experience. Think about it. When was the last time you were fully conscious of what you felt and how you were affecting others in each moment while you were with them? Work on this and the results come.

In front of an audience? Be a version of you (it doesn't have to be you entirely). Remember, all the world is a stage, and we are merely players etc. etc. It's a role you are playing, truthfully. It's a performance. A role where you allow your relevant appropriate feelings and emotions to be present in each moment when speaking.

The fundamental skills necessary for this aren't complicated. As I have mentioned, all this is common sense, stuff you already do. It is to simply breathe. Breathing into the body. But to breathe, you need to pause. A pause scares people because it screams the truth. Breathe fully into your diaphragm. And when you begin to focus on thoughts and feeling that do not serve you, like *What do they think of me?*, *They're not listening to me!*, *They're going to find me out*, *My mouth is getting dry*, and every other unhelpful thought you have when speaking, pause and breathe.

This simple and most obvious skill we have, that we deploy every millisecond of the day without conscious thought, has powerful ramifications for your presence. Use the breathing exercise to train your body to breathe with the belly automatically. Not to sound like a stuck record, but this is mindfulness in action.

The irony is, to be able to use emotion effectively and appropriately to connect with others (and we do need our emotions to connect), you need to do some thinking first.

Often, I find clients saying, *How could I have been so stupid?*, *What was I thinking?* I have, with kindness of course, said, *You weren't*. That's the problem. Being mindful (which is simply paying attention) isn't about getting rid of thinking. We're human; we're going to think. It's about giving space to your thoughts and choosing the right thought to help you drive the right emotional response. In a public speaking context, it is pausing to breathe, which gives you time to think, and in turn this provides you with an opportunity to choose the right, most appropriate emotion to bring to bear which will have an impact on your audience. The same practice applies to any form of speaking: in meetings, one-to-ones, and in the kitchen at home.

For me, this attitude of pausing, which is letting go, was a cardinal sin because it suggested passivity. Yet, more often than not, it has been the best course of action. I know when I have pushed too hard at a problem or a situation, I have made things worse. It has closed down my mind and prevented me from thinking creatively, and instead, I have driven myself round in ever-decreasing and exhausting circles. It the antithesis of *yes...and*.

Ever lost your keys? And the more you ruminate about where they are the less likely you are to find them.

Recently, I spoke to a room filled with successful business folk. I was bricking it. I think I was just having one of those days. Nothing was going the way I wanted it to. I broke down on the A3 and had to get the AA out to tow me to the venue. They fixed the car, but I was late. I realised I had left half the workbooks for the audience at home. Winner! I thought it may be a good idea to just sit in the car a moment. Hell, I was late anyway, another five minutes wasn't going to hurt. The pause I had before bolting into the venue and frantically hurtling through my talk was the best thing I did. It reminded me about the power of a pause. I was able to change the direction of my thinking. My pause wasn't passive, it was very much an active part of me and that present moment.

Taking an improv troupe around the country, playing in student unions, pubs, clubs, and fringe theatres was such fun and a lot of hard work. *Your Line or Mine?* was one of our shows – yip, just like the television series, you know the one. One Saturday evening in Belfast, there were about seven of us improvisers. The high-energy show ran like Usain Bolt on speed.

In the middle of a scene, there were four improvisers playing. A fifth improviser walked on stage silently. The others didn't notice him. He said nothing. He just stood there. Motionless. His motionless body language had power. He drew the audience's attention toward him. They began to wonder why he was there. What was going to happen next? He had more influence over the audience than the prevailing scene. Saying nothing, just standing. Tension built. Our non-verbal communication has immense clout.

Malcolm is a CEO of multi-national bank based in the UK. He is always having to speak to groups of employees from fifty to three hundred and fifty at any given time, and at the drop of a hat. Being at ease and being seen as a genuine safe pair of hands is crucial for re-building trust.

He speaks almost as fast has he can run. He used to be a hundred-metre specialist when he was at college. Never pausing. Believing people have to feel your passion for the subject, and a good way to get passion across is to speak quickly. In truth, Malcolm isn't wrong. Injecting pace can create a sense of excitement and passion. But not continuously for fifteen-twenty minutes.

Recently he told me, "*I can't get over the power I feel I have when using my breath as an anchor and pausing as a way to stop. It is so obviously physically to me now. It wasn't before. I am aware of it now. I can choose the pace I want."*

"What else have you noticed about your breath?"

"It's silly, but I am less conscious of my nerves. I know they are there, but they don't control me. I let the thoughts about them go. To your point, Deon, I am more present. More mindful."

"What effect have you noticed this has on the audience?"

"Well, quite a few people came up to me today to express their excitement about the project. They said it was down to the way I had pitched it this morning. They complimented me on galvanising the team. I am so better able to notice when I am pacing up and down, and when I can best move with an intent. I love it. What you have done for me in four hours no-one has ever been able to help me with in the twenty-five years I have been in banking."

Wow, shit the bed (obvs thought to myself). What a thing to say. But in truth, Malcolm would pace feverishly up and down the stage, his physical body movements mirroring his pace of delivering the words. No room for emotion at all. On the one hand, dare I say, it was all congruent – it meshed neatly together. But it didn't serve him or his audience. To be clear, we did not change his behaviour by numbers – purely looking at the external behaviours. We started with *why*. He got clear on an intent he could use repeatedly (I disagreed with this, but hey, you can't win every battle, so long as you win the war in the end) to drive his emotion and behaviour from a point of connectedness.

I asked him to undertake a regular practice. Ah, there's that word again. Practice – try, try, and try. If at first, and all that. His regular practice included letting his body do the talking to help him become more aware of how he used his body to convey trust, freeing himself up to use it in better ways that served his purpose.

A great big part of mastering this presence malarkey is becoming more conscious of self. Noticing bodily sensations and your responses to these physical sensations. In time, this awareness will develop into an unconscious competence of the effect your body can have on your ability to connect with others. It's going to sound a little wanky, but through the medium of self-observation, I can alter my energy state from one where things are small and intermit to something much larger. I am present. I have *a* presence in both these states. I am mindfully watching myself and others. It's important to remove judgement and criticism. When you do, you open up. You experience possibilities you may never have realised.

The other day, William and I were playing with his Lego. We were building a Lego city. Of course, I have my way; I'm Dad. William had a little outburst. He got upset that I had taken some of the pieces he decided he wanted. My response was, "*But you hadn't told me you wanted these pieces.*" He got really upset to the point of tears. Within moments, the situation had calmed down. I helped him see there were plenty more similar pieces. From that moment, he had a different state of mind. He had moved from being upset to joy and excitement. There was no hanging onto the past.

Equally, I have noticed when I have mentioned a list of things we are going to do in the day that he never questions why or when we are going to do the next things whilst he is playing with something else. I am not suggesting he forgets about going swimming later; I am saying when he is playing Lego, he is playing Lego. When he is playing *Top Trumps*, he is doing only that. He is present. He possesses a clarity of mind that says *I am, now.*

He has the emotion and then moves on. He is a master of detachment. He is only present. We then begin to fill him (them, our children) with all manner of thought and feeling, and they begin to develop that unhelpful worry about the past and concern for the future. They lose sight of their natural ability to be present. But we can remember. We can all experience the energy that is to be present. When we do, people notice it. Notice you. We can be truthfully charismatic.

Think about the last time you watched someone on stage give a talk. What was it that made you want to listen? What was it that made you want to hear everything they said? Setting the subject matter aside; that's just content. I bet there was an energy the person possessed. Not necessarily a nuclear-watt reactor type energy. A *measured-ness.* A clarity of mind and body. An assurance of *I am, now.* An ease. I have no doubt they projected an air of confidence, and we all experience that as *wow, they know their stuff.* It is the simplicity of intention, the use of intuition, and the acceptance of gratitude that brings about a sense of knowing yourself, trusting yourself, being yourself. That is true presence.

There's so much emphasis on being positive all the time. *We're all doing great. Everything's going to be successful.* But I think to myself, no. One has to experience the fears and negative emotions. You have to give yourself space to have the emotion. It's okay to panic and have that emotion as long as you don't get attached to it. You need to give yourself the space to have that emotion because everything can't be positive all the time because it's not real. As equally, everything can't be negative all the time because it's so consuming. Everything is about experience, therefore experience the emotion.

The Practice: Circles of Being

Noticing your energy, body language, thinking, and emotion can have an impact on people moment to moment and day to day. Notice how you can alter your energy and move through each circle in any conversation.

Circles of Being is used to master your ability to connect authentically with the thoughts and feelings of your audience. It is a technique used to develop a *state of being* through which you can influence your audience. It is an energy which fuels a certain kind of performance, presence, way of being.

Next time you are preparing a talk, presentation, just going into a meeting, or even having a conversation at home, play around with your personal energy. Explore the affect you can have on an audience by altering your energy moment to moment. Moving through first circle to third circle.

Circles of Being can help you live your purpose by showing up intentionally in each moment. Remember, practice detachment. Have the intention and then let it happen.

First Circle: Your focus is innermost, it is intimate. We usually reserve this type of energy for one-to-one conversations. Your voice is quiet, and your body is still and unaffected. It is almost as though you are speaking to yourself. It is very personal. It can be used to create a sense of curiosity. It is introspective and enticing. At its worst, you may be seen as hiding your presence away inside you. Too much first circle will diminish the perception of your presence, looking nervous or not confident.

The trick is being able to be in first when in front of a large audience as the expectation is you must be large and *out there*. Imagine drawing people in, your voice soft and relaxed. I see first as a way of quietly, warmly, and personally bonding with an audience. You can hear a pin drop. Create those moments.

Second Circle: You are fully present; you are in the moment. Your focus is placed outside yourself. You speak to affect others. As a speaker and leader, you require presence; second gives this. Here, you connect with people. It is our most common state. In second, you make a true connection and hold the audience rapt because they know you are truly present and entirely connected to them. However, it can be challenging to stay in second all the time, we're not the Dalai Lama. So be okay with moving into first and third as appropriate.

Third Circle: You are much bigger, bolder. Your movement is intentionally larger and perhaps audacious. You demonstrate concepts and ideas or stories with grand physical movements, and your voice is congruent to this. There is a self-assuredness in your voice. Third can become a generalised connection outward but not specifically to a person. When used in large spaces, this can have an impact.

The temptation whenever you speak is to become wrapped up in what you are doing and saying, but your performance takes on a whole different level when you start noticing the affect you have on yourself and the world around you.

Reflection Questions/Points:

1. What have you noticed about the way you move and use your body?
2. What have you noticed about the way others use their bodies?
3. What have you noticed about your personal energy – your presence? How does your ability to alter it feel to you?
4. What impact has your ability to choose your state of being had on the way you think or feel about yourself?
5. Where might you use some of this new-found awareness to your advantage when speaking and/or leading a team?

Remember to feed-forward:

Ask yourself...

- What did I do well when speaking that I should do more of?
- What could I do to improve next time?
- What am I grateful for in myself?

I Am Grounded in the Knowledge That I Know Why I Am Here

The other day, Dawn sent me Facebook message. She was having what we'd all call a 'bad day'. She was a little down about how some people had been responding to her via email in relation to an event she was organising. *"They just don't get it. I'm doing this for them. What's the point, Deon?"* We chatted about it on messenger.

As it happened, Dawn and I met up the next day. There we were in the pub, and the previous day's subject rose its ugly head. We started chewing the fat, talking about life and the meaning thereof. A lovely, light-hearted subject on a Friday afternoon. Dawn asked, *"When do we truly know ourselves? How do you know you are being yourself?"* I looked at her. I like to think I wasn't looking blankly at her. We'd had a glass of wine each by this point.

I corroborated her seemingly desperate feeling for answer by asking, *"What really do we know about anything? Why are we here?"* There was this long pause. I think we may have looked up and seen a hottie walking by. Good distraction. Present-moment detachment. And then came my response: *"When I've lived my life driven by curiosity, I have been conscious of an inner freedom and peace. I have only known two perspectives. One, living without purpose for over twenty years, which isn't living.*

And two, living with purpose. Living with purpose drives inquisitiveness and it dilutes fear."

Living into and through my purpose is about being intentional and intuitive, and it requires gratitude to experience it.

Emma and I decided, after being jobbing actors, that it would be a good idea to set up a theatre company. I had been working as an actor for almost five years when Emma and I met in the summer of 2004. I'd just got back from the European tour with *Oliver Twist*. Emma and I met doing a six-week improv tour around London. It was such a laugh. It was one of those acting jobs they advertise as 'profit share'. The advert should have read, *Blood, sweat, and tears. No money. Nothing!*

We set up Abandon Theatre. The definition of 'abandon' we liked was 'free from inhibition', and that became our strapline. Abandon Theatre, freedom from inhibition. Emma, Annalea, and I came up with it when we were out one night at the Kazbar or the Two Brewers.

Initially, there were five of us involved in Abandon Theatre, and we each put £50 in. We had no idea how to run a theatre company, and all we had was £250. But it was really exciting. We could do this. It felt right.

We ran Abandon Theatre because we wanted to put on theatre; we just wanted to do. Lots of people set up theatre companies because they want to make a political statement, or they want to do Shakespeare, or they want to change the world, or help disabled young people, which is brilliant. But none of that was relevant for us. We wanted to put on theatre because we wanted to. And I think that's the epicentre of life. We should just have the motivation to do for the sake of doing. To experience being. There's such contentment and joy in the moment of being. In the moment, when you're doing, you feel content because you have a purpose. It's not about the outcome; it's about the experience.

We believed we could be everything to everyone all at the same time, so we wanted to do theatre for theatre's sake, we wanted to do improvisation, and we realised we needed to make money, so we had to do presentation skills training. And then we got asked whether we would come in and do mediation training. What the fuck? I'm not a mediator. We were then asked if we would come in and create a programme of training for middle managers to help them get better at managing conflict.

Because I was in HR, I thought I was able to write proposals for funding. This was another way to get money. But the thing is, that funding only comes if you do the work for community groups. So we got lots of funding, but we ended up doing community theatre, which is great for the community, but it wasn't what we were focused on or wanted to do. There was no clear purpose.

We had no money, and we were driven by the desire to do do do do and get whatever we could, and sometimes we were standing up there improvising. But Emma and I were good at that, and people bought into us. But we'd become everything to everybody and nothing to ourselves. We lost sight of who we were. Maybe we were driven by this freedom of inhibition. Either way, there wasn't a clear focus – a clear purpose.

Because we were everything to everyone, Emma and I were producers, directors, organisers, and actors. But all we wanted to do was perform. So we were faced with the challenge of working out what role to play. What would I be best at? Where would I add the most value? And I've always grappled with that. I was everything to everybody, but I wasn't something to myself.

We needed purpose and intent, and because we didn't have that, we found ourselves trying to do too much for too many people. We'd forgotten that we started Abandon Theatre because we wanted to do theatre. We wanted to go out and do. We'd forgotten our intent.

Over the Years, There's Been an Explosion of Interest in Purpose-Driven Leadership

People argue persuasively that a CEO or MD's most important role is to be a steward of the organisation's purpose. Business experts make the case that purpose is a key to exceptional performance, while psychologists describe it as the pathway to greater well-being. Doctors have even found that people with purpose in their lives are less prone to disease. Purpose is increasingly being touted as the key to navigating the complex, volatile, ambiguous world we face today, where strategy is ever-changing, and few decisions are obviously right or wrong. Despite this growing understanding, however, a big challenge remains.

I've found that fewer than 20% of leaders have a strong sense of their own individual purpose. Even fewer can distil their purpose into a concrete statement. They may be able to clearly articulate their organisation's mission: think of Google's, *to organize the world's information and make it universally accessible and useful.* But when asked to describe their own purpose, they typically fall back on generic and nebulous statements such as *Help others excel, Ensure success, Empower my people.* And hardly any of them have a clear plan for translating purpose into action. As a result, they limit their aspirations and often fail to achieve their most ambitious professional and personal goals. My purpose is to change that.

Living my purpose gives me direction. I am grounded in the knowledge that I know why I am here. I know why I do the things I do. I know I am being me. Living my purpose gives me the freedom to create deep, trusting connections with people, including clients, my team, and family. I am content. I am happy. Living my purpose has been the pathway to exceptional performance and greater well-being. And I know I will have the impact my heart desires and leave a legacy. But it wasn't always like this.

I help executives find and define their leadership purpose and put it to use. I help them find, speak, and live their purpose. I believe that the process of articulating your purpose and finding the courage to live it is the single most important developmental task you can undertake as a leader. Here is a simple step-by-step framework to start you down the path of finding, speaking, and living your purpose, and then develop a plan to achieve concrete results.

What is Your Purpose?

Your leadership purpose is who you are and what makes you distinctive. It is the essence of you. Whether you're an entrepreneur at a start-up or the CEO of a multi-national corporation, a call centre rep or a software developer, your purpose is your brand, the magic that makes you tick. It's not *what* you do, it's *how* you do your job and live your life and *why*. It is the strengths and passions you bring to the table no matter where you're seated. Although you may express your purpose in different ways in different contexts, it's what everyone close to you recognises as uniquely you and would miss most if you were gone. Finding, speaking, and living your true purpose will enhance your trustworthiness. When you:

1. Find your story – it gives you a freedom to create deep, emotion-fuelled, and trusting connections with your audience.
2. Lead and live with purpose – this is the pathway to exceptional performance and greater well-being.
3. Leave your legacy – by planting the seeds that grow consistency and expectations, which become the funnel for future exceptional performance.

There is a seven-step process to finding your purpose and building a plan for speaking and living it. They are explained in more detail later on.

Step One – Mining your life stories looking for common threads and major themes.

Step Two – Unpicking your most challenging life experiences.

Step Three – Knowing what is important to you.

Step Four – Singing your song.

Step Five – Writing your purpose statement and its explanation.

Step Six – Speaking it, finding out what others think.

Step Seven – Building your purpose into your 1-3-5 plan, setting goals and building relationships to live it.

The Truth of Leadership is to Know Yourself, Trust Yourself, and Be Yourself

Jeanette and I moved to Northern Ireland in 1994. We moved because we wanted to see other parts of the world. But that was bollocks. I moved because I thought I could run away from the lies I'd created. I wanted to run away from the sexual abuse too. I just wanted to be in a different place. We didn't go fucking travelling.

I never believed that South Africa was part of me. I didn't fit into that way of life. I wonder how long I would've stayed married if we hadn't left. Would I have ever come to a point where I came out and was able to be myself? I think I probably would've stayed married. If I did eventually come out, I think it would've been much, much later.

Leaving South Africa was the best thing to do, certainly for me. I don't think I would be as content with things as I am had I not left. When you are trapped on a continent consumed by its bigotry you see a freedom in the Northern hemisphere.

Jeanette and I moved to Northern Ireland because a friend of mine from Northern Ireland was going back, and I thought, *fuck, this is a great opportunity*. We arrived on the thirty-first of March 1994. It was pissing with rain and freezing cold. I thought, *what the fuck have I done?* It was awful. It was a long flight. We had a shower and got into bed, and we lay in bed and cried together. We said we're going back home to South Africa. We said we'd stay there for a holiday, but we'd go back to South Africa. But we ended up enjoying ourselves. It's a great country.

Jeanette had to go back South Africa to finish teaching, and we said we'd talk more and decide whether we were going to leave or stay once she came back. But I decided I was going to stay. I started seeing men and recreating the same shit I had left in South Africa. I couldn't trust myself.

We were apart for about six months, and we wrote to each other every single day. The commonality of our bond, growing up in South Africa, and the fact she left her parents for me is what made our relationship work. We were young, little kindred spirits. But our bond was peppered with lies, deceit, and untruths.

I decided not to teach in Northern Ireland. I had loads of other jobs. I changed jobs like I changed my underwear. I'd get to the top and then leave. I was the best salesperson in the sports chain I worked in before leaving South Africa. I was then the head of the region, and I created this whole training programme for in-house sports advisors. I was sought after. But I didn't want to do it. It was shit, and I hated it. Eventually, I just stopped bothering with it. My performance dipped, and the district manager came to talk to me. He asked me what'd happened, and I just looked him in the eyes and said, "*I don't want to do this fucking crap any more. I think it's a load of shit. I'm leaving.*" And I got up, and I walked out. And that's what I did regularly, in this dramatic fashion. I decided I was going to do something, but I didn't really want to do it. I decided I was going to perform, but then fuck it, I couldn't be arsed. Always searching for something outside of me.

The same thing happened with swimming. Mrs Palmer said I was going to be amazing, that I would qualify for South African Nationals. Then I was beaten by one hundredth of a second, and that was that. Fuck you. Can't be arsed. It was the same with the businesses Emma and I have had. There's a pattern. And all the while, through all of those things, the reason was because I wasn't being true to myself. At the end of the day, truth works.

At its core, your leadership purpose springs from your identity, the essence of who you are. Purpose is not a list of the education, experience, and skills you've gathered in your life. Let me use an example. The fact that Martin is managing director of multi-million-pound manufacturing business in the UK is not his purpose. His purpose is *to explore and be curious, helping others to do the same.* Purpose is also not a professional title limited to your current job or organisation. My purpose is not *to lead our company, Truth.Works. and the brand to global success.* That's my job.

Purpose is definitely not some jargon-filled catch-all (*Empower my team to achieve exceptional business results while delighting our customers*). It should be specific and personal, resonating with you and you alone. It doesn't have to be aspirational or cause-based (*Save the whales* or *Feed the hungry*). And it's not what you think it should be. It's who you can't help being. In fact, it might not necessarily be all that flattering (*Be the thorn in people's side that keeps them moving!*).

In Northern Ireland, I happened to go and perform

in an interview for a company called Olympus Sports. I talked about how I had worked in HR and personnel in a previous role in South Africa. So I ended up with this incredible role, and I was paid £25,000 a year, and to me in 1995, that was millions. I was the HR director for a hundred and fifty staff in this huge out of town store in Lisburn. Way out of my depth. Hugely out of my depth. But I was great at creating relationships and getting people to work together, and the store performed exceptionally well. I'm someone who's always made people work well for themselves and for others. But I was really shit at all the administration. I left all the banking and administration for six months, and I got fired. Although, before I got fired, I resigned. I did the same thing that I always did. I had a huge argument with the district manager, and I said, *"Fuck you."* And I just walked out. I didn't know myself.

After that, Jeanette said I needed to go and speak to someone about the sexual abuse. She didn't like how negative and consuming the homophobia was for me. As the reluctant performer, I found that yes, I wanted to, but no, I didn't, all at the same time. So I started by going to the doctor with Jeanette, and they recommended a counsellor. It was the beginning of the end for Jeanette and me when she encouraged me to go and see someone. It was the start of doing right by me, of me chipping away at autopilot living and stepping into being. Although it would be some time before I lived my true purpose.

My first councillor looked like Dolores Umbridge from *Harry Potter*. That was the counsellor they referred me to. I mean, how could I relate to her? I just lied. I perpetuated the lie. I didn't talk to her about the sexual abuse. I went through six or seven different people until eventually I found this organisation called Nexus, and I started to go and see a counsellor. I started talking to him and telling him about it all.

The truth of leadership is to know yourself, trust yourself, and be yourself; only then will you be truly trustworthy. Finding your purpose is not easy. If it were, we'd all know exactly why we're here and be living that purpose every minute of every day. And let's face it, we are constantly bombarded by powerful messages (from parents, bosses, management gurus, advertisers, celebrities) about what we should be (smarter, stronger, richer) and about how to lead (empower others, lead from behind, be authentic, distribute power). To figure out who you are in such a world, let alone *be nobody but yourself*, is indeed hard work. However, my experience shows that when you have a clear sense of who you are, everything else follows naturally.

The seven-step process will be very different from person to person. Some of you might be naturally bent towards introspection and self-reflection. Others will find the experience disruptive, challenging, uncomfortable, and anxiety-provoking. Others of you may even just roll your eyes – you may be doing this now. But it works, it really does. I've worked with leaders of all stripes and can attest that even the most sceptical discover personal and professional value in the experience.

Adventure is the Reason I Like Baking

This morning I was taking William to football practice. School holidays. I had a business client call to take at ten o'clock sharp. I hated having these calls. Not because they were business calls, but because I had to use a meeting dial-in thingy. You know the kind where you have a pin number to key in after you dial the official number of the meeting provider. It never works properly. Well, for me at least. Technology and me are like oil and water.

So there I was dropping William off amongst eighty other kids. So mayhem. I was hurrying things along, going over instructions to him, kissing him goodbye, and still trying to be affectionate, but at the same time feeling anxious about getting out of there and somewhere plausible for a business phone call. My emotions ebbed and flowed from anxiety and fear to joy and pleasure (whilst hugging and kissing him); my emotions we driven by circumstance.

If I am brutally honest, there are many occasions where feelings or emotions of this kind come up for me. Some far more intense than others. My responses in situations have helped define certain habits. I believe we cannot escape this, be it a child on the playground responding to bullying or a leader of global business or nation dealing with rejection or success. Every single human event is shaped by our emotional experiences. And when we retell it, we create a narrative or story filled with emotions as we see them. This is useful for communicating with others. It is human. We all experience this, but we are not the sum of our emotional responses. Our habits.

Knowing is nothing without change. Knowing is nothing without implementation. Clarifying your purpose as a leader is critical, but so too is envisioning the impact you'll have on your world through living your purpose. You know your actions – not your words – are what really matter. Of course, it's virtually impossible for any of us to fully live our purpose 100% of the time. But with work and careful planning, we can do it more often, more consciously, wholeheartedly, and effectively.

Margaret Thatcher, in the film *The Iron Lady* recited the powerful and insightful words (attributed to many, including St Frances of Assisi)

> *"Watch your thoughts, for they become words. Watch your words, for they become actions. Watch your actions, for they become habits. Watch your habits, for they become your character. And watch your character, for it becomes your destiny."*

All living things have dispositions or tendencies to respond to things in certain ways. Just as a flower has an inherent disposition to lean towards the sun, and birds and butterflies are disposed to fly. Human beings have dispositions to respond emotionally. We sometimes don't even notice our emotions, or that they are being drawn out from us constantly.

Our emotions sway back and forth depending on what

we are encountering. When we experience something pleasurable, we then feel pleasure. When we do something frightening, we subsequently feel fearful. When we argue in our relationships, this can make us feel despair, or if we are livid with a friend, this can arouse jealousy. When we walk into that boardroom with dread, we feel the anxiousness. When we stand up and present to large auditorium, we may experience calmness because we see ourselves having a conversation. Or the complete opposite; we experience an inner turmoil because we have had this experience often and it has not gone well. These reoccurring experiences feed us signals that tell us to respond in a certain fashion. So we do. Our responses then become our habits.

I have a habit not only for seeing in people their true nature; I have a habit of seeing the adventure in being. Perhaps that's why I'm okay with a blank canvas. Okay with change. Okay with starting again. Seeing the opportunity.

We put on some brilliant shows as Abandon Theatre, and they started out as blank canvases. Emma and I did a devised piece together, and it was one of the best shows we did. We got great reviews; we loved it. I've always loved creating something from nothing. I think that is one of the biggest drivers behind me as a person: seeing things as an adventure, as an opportunity to create. The businesses are an example of that. They were opportunities to create something from nothing, and whilst there were loads of shows that we did in Abandon Theatre, I think the most enjoyable piece was that we were creating something. It was an adventure. Fraught with possible danger, good and bad emotions, ups and downs, and a shitload of uncertainty. Improv is like that. Leadership is too. Hell, life is.

It takes more than twenty-one days to form a habit, and to know yourself, trust yourself and be your true self you have to start forming new habits. There are things you have got to be doing regularly.

Maxwell Maltz was a famous plastic surgeon working in the 1950s. When he performed an operation, like a nose job, he found that it would take his patient a minimum of twenty-one days to get used to seeing their new face. Or when a patient had an amputation, Maltz noticed that the patient would sense a phantom limb for a minimum of twenty-one days before adjusting to the new situation. Do you know where this story is going? Fast-forward a few decades, and this twenty-one-day habit-forming phenomenon has become ingrained in our collective brain. People forgot that he said a *minimum* of twenty-one days and shortened it to *it takes twenty-one days to form a new habit.*

Don't get drawn in by this myth. It's remarkable how often these timelines are quoted as statistical facts. It makes sense why the twenty-one days myth took hold. It's easy to understand. The timeframe is short enough to seem achievable but long enough to be believable. Who wouldn't like the idea of changing your life in just three weeks? Remember, Rome wasn't built in a day.

What's the real answer? How long does it take to form a new habit? And is there any science to back this up? Philippa Lally is a health psychology researcher at University College London. She suggests that on average it takes *more* than two months before a new behaviour starts to feel normal. How long it takes a new habit to form can vary widely depending on the individual behaviour, the person, and the circumstances. The truth is, it'll probably take you anywhere from two to eight months to begin to form new memories about finding your truth, speaking it, using it in different circumstances, and living it.

So, Emma and I did this devised two-hander play about two people who were friends. Over the course of six months, we would improvise scenes. We would have conversations as two people who were married, and then we would try two people who were friends but hadn't seen each other for twenty years, then we would try and have dialogue between two people who were brother and sister. Eventually, one particular path stuck, and we developed and grew and built on that. We built new habits. That's what rehearsal does.

For me, that kind of work, that kind of blank canvas, is such an adventure, such an exciting way of operating, of being. We didn't know where we were going, but the purpose was to find out.

The adventure of uncertainty is why I've survived. I like not knowing exactly where things are going. But I get it; in business that's not enough. There must be a plan. There must be an ultimate purpose.

We find ourselves experiencing certain emotions more often than we do others, and our responses then become our habits. This is what life is about – moment after moment in which people encounter one another reacting in an infinite number of ways and pulled to and fro emotionally. Human life consists of people constantly bumping up against one another and reacting passively. We live in a fragmented world. One in which we are buffeted about endlessly by disparate events.

I think adventure is the reason I like baking. People think baking is very prescriptive and all about following the recipe. It is to a point. But I say fuck that, usually. We learn through doing. Even when I make cupcakes with William, we don't follow a recipe. Well, they're simple to make. And now he knows, because we've made cupcakes I don't know how many times, that in order to make twelve cupcakes, we need 180g of self-raising flour, 180g of unsalted butter, etc. He knows all of it, and he's learnt it without ever seeing the recipe. He's learnt it by doing. We've formed the right habits. Which is a little metaphor in a way for what Emma and I do. We don't follow a recipe to help you be who you truly are. We just know.

Creativity always starts with doing, with getting up on your feet, which is what I always tell my clients. You need to experience it. Rehearse it. Practice it. You need to try it out, feel what's right, hear what it sounds like. It's the same in theatre, and it's the same in business.

Before we took *Your Line or Mine?* to Edinburgh, we staged Ryan J-W Smith's *Sweet Love Adieu*. A spoof of *Romeo and Juliet* written in iambic pentameter. Love it! I had to put on thirty pounds to play Lord Edmund. Oh, method actor babe, totes method.

We decided in the first year of the theatre company, with no money, that we would take a ten-member cast to Edinburgh, pay for the accommodation, and pay for their travel. We said it was profit share, which meant no one made any money. But we were the best reviewed show in our venue. It was great. We ended up with £20,000 worth of debt though, so we had to try and get work to pay it off. That's how we first started at a global engineering firm, which was one of our very first clients.

Karen, one of our actresses, was a receptionist at the firm and was out one night with the senior partners, pissed, and they said they needed someone to help with their presentation skills training, and she said she knew some people. So she introduced us. Emma and I went to meet Richard, senior partner, with our shittest business cards. We'd never pitched for business in our lives. But I'm all about doing. What an adventure. I had no idea what kind of presentation skills thing we would do, but we just went in to listen and respond. Improvise.

We sat there, and Richard said, *"I'll give you guys a go. You do a day with me and my senior partners, there are eight of us, and I'll pay you 50% upfront. If you're great, you can work with all the senior team, but if you're shit, you'll never work again in London."* So we said okay, let's do it, and we worked with the senior executives of the firm for maybe eight years. We just went ahead and did it.

I can recall a time when I wasn't able to escape a bad habit. We took *Your Line or Mine?* to Edinburgh and had an incredible run. We used to do 'pay what you think it's worth' nights to promote it, and two actors would stand with hats at the end of the performance and people would put money in them. We made more money doing that than getting people to buy tickets.

While we were there, I had a fall out with one of the actors. Let's just call it artistic differences. My usual bad habit was to shut down and not engage. It took some shock-therapy from my friend Annalea to sort me out. *Deon, stop being a knob!*

I think we can all too easily get caught up in habits we believe serve us, and when we are able to see (or in my case are shown by others), we can live purposefully. We find our true nature. The essence of me. It's funny I've always known why I'm here, I was just too afraid to live it. Unwilling to clarify it for fear of what I might need to change to live it. This time I needed someone to help me see. Because of it, I was able to redefine me.

We are not the sum of our emotional responses. We can, with practice, choose the intensity of these emotions. We can choose the emotion we wish to bring to bear too. And when we do, we can change our habits. Then we live truthfully.

The Practice: Rehearsal

Change a habit of a lifetime. Next time you have a meeting or a pitch or talk or presentation to do, prepare it using the practice guides in this book. But make sure you do one of the most important pieces of preparation. Rehearsal. Practice the habit of being confident by rehearsing your content out loud.

Give yourself permission to do this. You will be amazed at the results. Remember to have an intent and a call-to-action and use a story from your River of Life.

Remember to feed-forward:

Ask yourself…

1. What did I do well that I should do more of?
2. What could I do to improve next time?
3. What am I grateful for in myself?

The Key to Engaging Both the Dreamers and the Sceptics is to Live as You

Every month like clockwork I have my regular coach supervision session. It's an hour of me essentially talking at Steve about everything and anything concerning my practice of helping CEOs get to grips with who they are and more besides. I love my sessions with Steve. Steve is probably the only person on the planet that knows every thought in my head before I do. Although, as ever, just before the session, I thought to myself, *can I not just get on with what I must do today!* In this session, I noticed I was a lot more reluctant to talk than usual. I tried not to rationalise it, just let it happen. I trusted the relationship. I trusted him and myself. I am my true self when talking to him.

What I noticed was this foot-dragging to talk about clients. I am a dreamer and sceptic all rolled into one. Ying and yang. For Christ sake, I'm Pisces, two fish swimming in opposite directions. One minute I do, the next, nah, fuck it. This morning, I just wasn't in the mood. We laughed about it. I asked, *"Have I told you about the book?"* *"No,"* was his reply. *"Although I sensed you were writing something. Talk to me about the book."* I was apprehensive because I didn't know why I was doing it. Why should I talk about the book? Steve said, *"Just tell me a story in it, something that I don't know about you already."* I told him the army story. It was a brilliant coaching supervision session. I was given permission to live my purpose. I know the story changed something in him.

Your plan for living your purpose must start with a statement of leadership purpose rather than of a business or career goal. Take a complete view of your professional and personal life rather than ignore the fact that you have a family or outside interests and commitments. You need to use meaningful and motivational language to create a plan that speaks to you, not just to any person in your job or role.

My purpose and plan help me to stay true to my short- and long-term goals, inspiring courage, commitment, and focus. When I have been frustrated or flagging, I look at the plan to remind me of what I want to accomplish and how I will succeed.

Recently, a client of mine said, *"I no longer shy away from things that are too hard. I'm much clearer on where I really can contribute and where not. I have full clarity on the kind of roles I aspire to and can make explicit choices along the way."* Alistair and I have been working together for some six months. He attended our three-day residential programme, which we run six times a year. Finding his purpose and living and leading through it is important for Alistair. In our one-to-one sessions, Alistair and I were discussing his childhood passions. He told me about growing up near the English Welsh boarder and delighting in discovery missions with his best friend.

Every day they would be outdoors exploring, climbing through hedgerows and digging through mud and peat searching for life. One summer day, he and his friend set out determined to find frogs. They had a school project to complete and spent the whole day going from pond to pond, turning over every stone. Just before Alistair knew he had to go home, they discovered a single frog and were triumphant. Alistair is the CEO of an international ecosystem research firm. He uncovered his purpose statement – *Always find the frogs!* – and it is perfect for him, his business, and his life's purpose. The qualification statement is: *Never leaving any stone unturned.*

We all live and work from a slightly different set of assumptions about the world, different industries, what can or can't be done. I know my individual perspective allows me to create great value and have significant impact. You too can live by your unique leadership purpose. I believe the truth of leadership is to know yourself, trust yourself, and be yourself; only then will you be truly trustworthy. To be a truly effective leader, you must do the same. Clarify your purpose and put it to work.

The key to engaging both the dreamers and the sceptics is to live as you. The process I suggest to you has room for you to express your individuality but also offers step-by-step practical guidance.

I've taken some time to figure out how best to live as me. After I left the army, Jeanette and I lived together in Benoni, and all the while I had this turmoil and tussle with my duty as a husband and my want to fulfil that, and this wrath of God in my head. I wanted to fulfil my duty as a husband, and I wanted to *want* to fulfil that. I wanted to have a family and be like we were in Zimbabwe when I was younger. I thought I would create this life for us and live this lie for the rest of my life. I never wanted to upset anybody.

But what I was doing was going off cottaging and having sordid experiences wherever I could find other men. It was this dirty kind of sex and interaction that I associated with Gary. So on the one hand, I wanted to do the right thing, but I was lying and cheating. But I used to tell myself I wasn't cheating because I wasn't doing it with a woman. Funny how we can convince ourselves of something. I did that for most of our marriage; 90% I'd say. I didn't when we were at college, when we were courting, but when we got married, I did.

Our relationship was the envy of all our friends. We had this incredible trust and understanding, but it was built on lies. For me, that says something about leaders in business. Build a house on truth, and it breeds trust, and it will stand. But build your house on a series of lies and untruths about who you are, and it will all fall apart as it did for me.

I trust you have completed your River of Life. In there, you will find the answers to the questions in each step.

I suggest that you complete the following exercise with a trusted colleague. Do it together. An effective way to approach this exercise is to ask your colleague these questions and write down their responses. Or attend one of our three-day residentials. Wink, wink, nudge, nudge. People come from all over the globe.

It's almost impossible for people to identify their leadership purpose by themselves. You can't get a clear picture of yourself without trusted colleagues or friends to act as mirrors. After this reflective work, take a shot at crafting a clear, concise, and declarative statement of purpose. The words in your purpose statement must be yours. They must capture your essence. Make sure it is short, snappy, and punchy. It must motivate you. It must call you to action. As you review your stories, you will see a unifying thread. Pull it, and you'll uncover your purpose.

Sarah, a serial entrepreneur and mother, used two significant life experiences to craft her purpose. The first was personal: years ago, as a divorced young mother of two, she found herself homeless and living on the street. Her children were taken into care. She was abusing drugs. She used her wits to get back on her feet. The second was professional: during the economic crisis of 2008, she had to oversee her company's liquidation. She was tasked with closing the flagship operation in the UK. Despite the near hopeless financial situation, she helped every one of her employees find another job before letting them go. Sarah explored these two key moments in her life and unpicked her true values. She shifted her purpose statement from, *Continually and consistently develop and facilitate the growth and development of myself and others leading to great performance* to *with tenacity, create brilliance*. She used the first statement to clarify her purpose.

Step One – What Did I Love Doing?

The first step in finding your purpose is to mine your life stories looking for common threads and major themes.

In pairs, explore your answers to the following question. The sub-questions are intended to help you delve deep.

What did you especially love doing when you were a child before the world told you what you should or

shouldn't like or do? Describe a moment and how it made you feel.

1. What resonates with you about this time?
2. If you could distil this experience down into a sentence (or a few words or phrases), what would it/ they be?
3. How do you feel right now telling others about this moment? Use three words ONLY.

Step Two – What Were My Challenges?

Tell us about two of your most challenging life experiences. How have they shaped you?

1. What are the lessons for you from these experiences that tell you something about who you are?
2. How does your handling of these experiences tell you what you are capable of?
3. How do you feel about these experiences? Use three words ONLY.

Step Three – What is Important to Me?

What is and has been important to you? List words and phrases that identify your values.

Identify three of the most important words or phrases from your list of answers to Step Three above. Consider and make notes about:

1. What story/stories from your past bring the value

to life?

2. Who was present in the story?
3. What happened in the story? What were the course of events that took place?
4. What feelings or emotions do you have/did you have about the story?
5. What was the lasting impression from the story?

Step Four – What Do I Enjoy Doing Now?

What do you enjoy doing in your life now that helps you sing your song?

1. What could be the possibilities if you purposefully sing your song?
2. When will you do more, to sing your song?
3. What will you do to ensure you sing your song purposefully?

Step Five – What is My Purpose?

Now that you've completed this reflective work, take a shot at crafting a clear, concise, and declarative statement of purpose.

The words in your purpose statement must be yours. They must capture your essence. And they must call you to action.

Follow up your purpose statement with an explanation of why this is your purpose.

Step Six – What Have I and Others Noticed?

Now speak your purpose. Share with your partner (in two minutes) one of your stories from Step Three and end your storytelling with your purpose statement.

1. How did it feel to talk about your purpose using this story?
2. Where might you be able to do this again?

Once you have completed the above, seek out others, e.g. colleagues, family members, and ask them if they think it fits. Use your stories from Step Three to frame your purpose statement.

You need to sit with your purpose statement for a few weeks. Over the next thirty days, notice in your everyday activity if you are 'being it' – living it. Review it again.

Step Seven – Living My Purpose!

Complete and implement a plan to live your purpose. Living your purpose is key to exceptional performance, and it is the pathway to greater well-being.

I like to keep things simple, mainly because I am so forgetful. I like to apply the 1-3-5 rule (Google it). It is an easy way to set a vision (1) for living your purpose. It asks you to identify core objectives (3) to help you achieve your vision and goals (5) for each of your three core objectives.

I use it to create an uncomplicated plan written for two-three years in the future written as though I have achieved it. I am already there.

I then set three core objectives aligned to help me

achieve my vision. I like finance and work, physical, mental and emotional well-being, and the third core objective is family and home. Then I set five goals for each of the three core objectives.

Here are some guidance questions to help you populate your 1-3-5:

1. **Vision**

Be specific and emotive about your vision. The focus should be on how you will *be* it and what kind of leader you'll be. These questions might help:

- What am I doing?
- Who am I with? What relationships are in my life? Who is there?
- Where am I living and working?
- What am I doing with my time? How much time is dedicated to the various aspects of my life?
- What is my purpose? And how does it help me achieve my vision? This must be explicitly visible in your vision.

Here is an example:

I run a globally recognised consultancy helping CEOs find, speak, and live their purpose, improving the lives of self and others. I do this by speaking globally (80% of my work time) and running week-long residential programmes abroad in my summer home in southern Spain.

I live my purpose – changing people, changing lives – spending eight months of the year focused on delivering my work objectives and goals, with August and

December each year off. I write, produce, and direct theatre productions in London. I holiday throughout the year with family and on my own. I spend 50% of time with William and David.

2. **Core Objectives**

Keep these specific. Short and sweet. Essentially, your core objectives and goals need to be SMART. The question to ask yourself here is: what do I need to do in relation to *family and home, finance and work, health and well-being* to help me achieve my vision?

Here is an example of my *finance and work* core objective:

I work with thirty individuals in twelve months helping them find, speak, and live their truth.

I know what this means for me financially. In other words, I know what I need to do to achieve this, but also how much income this means.

3. **Goals**

Again, in my experience, these must be specific. Using my *finance and work* core objective here are my goals:

- Speaking globally each month
- Six fully-booked residentials each year
- Directing and producing theatre
- Working one hundred and forty-six days in twelve months

The question to ask yourself here is: *How will I achieve my core objective?*

Then look at the **key relationships** needed to turn your plan into reality. Identify two or three people who can help you live your leadership purpose more fully.

Finally, each week I suggest setting a maximum of ten Very Important Tasks (VITs) that you will focus on. These VITs should help you achieve your goals for your 1-3-5.

Do Yourself a Favour and Look Up and Pay Attention

I live in South London. I regularly catch South West Trains into Waterloo station. It's throbbing with people all the time. One morning around half nine, I was listening to my favourite meditation app whilst looking out the window at the London skyline. I prefer looking up to looking down. I take in more this way.

The train pulled into platform twenty-two. Everybody started to pile out of the eleven-coach train. Hundreds of people. It's quite peculiar watching people in everyday, run-of-the-mill circumstances. There we all were walking towards the turnstiles at the end of the platform. Imagine a sea of people gushing towards the turnstiles. A wall of people moving towards the end of platform twenty-two. I noticed most people were congregating in a bunch, all huddled together like a swarm of bees with their heads down looking at their phones. All bunching behind a collection of turnstiles. But just to their right were half a dozen empty ones. No one noticed them.

The tensions and frustration started to build. You could taste the annoyance in the air. *Look up for a moment*, I thought to myself. When we do, we see opportunities and give ourselves permission to feel the freedom of taking an alternative route. I find it amusing. Why do we stick to a course when we know this course is not serving us? Why do we not use our intuition? Why do we live so mindlessly? When will we live intentionally and be open to our intuition for the peace and freedom this provides?

I know I sound rather melodramatic, but seriously! It's funny. Next time you take a train or a bus, do yourself a favour and look up and pay attention.

Starting a theatre company was one of the best adventures of my life. Not only was it fun and I was living my truth, it taught me a very valuable lesson. I started my conscious journey into awareness. Mindfulness. Being observant. Forming the *right* habits for me. And the simple but certainly most tricky habit of paying attention.

I'd always wanted to go to drama school, and when I had the opportunity, I went to Webber Douglas in London. Drama school essentially taught me how to pay attention. To be a good actor you must learn to observe. Notice what is happening around you – the external stimuli: the tone of voice, body language, actions, words and emotions of others – and recognise what is happening inside you – your response to the external stimuli. Mindfulness.

Mindfulness doesn't ask you to stop doing. Mindfulness asks you, *is this what you intend to do?* Mindful speaking and living asks you, *is this what you intended?* If not, choose an alternative. From a speaking perspective, this is extremely powerful. Imagine for a moment you are talking to a large auditorium of people. Hey, maybe it's a keynote. Or perhaps it's your board of directors. Imagine being able to choose how to be moment to moment when you stand up there. Not how to think; you do this automatically – you've spent your whole life building your capacity to assess, analyse, judge, and make assumptions. But imagine being able to choose alternatives to what is expected of you (from yourself and from others) in each moment.

A client once said to me, "*You and Emma are the directors, and we're the actors*", and that's a good analogy for what we do. The director's someone who helps the actor find the appropriate emotion to convey in a scene. The director is the one who helps the actor recognise which habits work best. The director helps the actor notice what he/she is experiencing. The director teaches the actor (through the rehearsal process) to learn to respond to that experience with relevant emotion. The latter is what the audience connects with. The same is said for connecting with the various audiences you speak to.

Drama school, and particularly improvisation, taught me to experience the moment. To begin to master the craft of paying attention, here are two brilliant questions to keep asking yourself as you go through every day. What am I experiencing now? How am I responding to this experience? Notice your thoughts, feelings, and physical sensations.

When Emma and I were working as improv actors, I remember one of the suggestions we got from an audience was, *you are in a nuclear bunker and you have to get out somehow*. We created the ninety-minute show that ebbed and flowed. It had real drama in it. For example: there was no way of getting out, and the oxygen was going to run out in an hour's time, and no one knew it, but someone found out.

It's about those two core skills of improv: listening and responding. To do this, you have to pay attention. Playing mindfully. Noticing what is happening around you and inside you. And then respond. Putting it another way, it is just being able to commit oneself fully to an experience.

The Practice: Ten Times Speed

Here is a brilliant exercise to bring this to life:

Get a few people together, people you trust. This is fun and a little wacky, but it works. Take a playful scenario, for example planning the office party. Plan it, discuss it, brainstorm it together at ten times the normal pace.

Everything has to be really fast so you don't have time to think about what comes next. Notice. What are you experiencing? What is happening around you? Let it happen. Don't try make it happen.

Reflection Questions/Points:

1. What did you notice about the way you contributed to the game?
2. What did you notice about your personal energy – your presence? How does your ability to alter it feel to you?
3. What messages did you pick up from others' non-verbal signals? What relevance does this have for you when speaking and leading?
4. What sensation did you notice for yourself? What do they tell you about what you were experiencing?
5. Where might you use some of this new-found

awareness to your advantage when speaking and/or leading a team?

Remember to feed-forward:

Ask yourself…

1. What did I do well that I should do more of?
2. What could I do to improve next time?
3. What am I grateful for in myself?

Consider a room full of senior engineers. Yes, mostly men. In fact, all men bar one. So there I was intending to help these senior executives pay attention to their intuition. Of course, I was brought in to do presentation skills training. But fuck, that wasn't what I had in store for them. They didn't know it either. The first thing I made them do was all shout out one after the other, "*I failed!*", and if I didn't believe they meant it – owned it – I got them to do it until they did. I then got them to stand in a circle with their backs to each other and try to count to twenty-one one at a time and without speaking over one another. If they did, they had to go back to the beginning. One guy decided he was going to stream-roller everyone and do it on his own. Knob.

Eventually, they got it. The crucial learning for them was their ability to be present, to notice, and what this felt like. They noticed physical sensations, emotions, and thoughts, which at first appeared to be distracting, not least of all their thinking how ridiculous and absurd this is. "*This noticing is it, gentlemen, and lady,*" I said. Being in a pressure situation and being able to notice.

I then got them to start passing an invisible ball around the circle and told them to face each other. Then I added another ball, and another, and finally a football. Twenty senior global executives in a room mastering their presentation skills by passing invisible balls around a circle. Lost the plot? No! What they all began to notice was their ability to pay attention to what they were experiencing.

They noticed after a little time had passed that they had all let go of the habit of wanting to be the best. They had all lost the embarrassed feelings. They had forgotten about competing with each other. Instead, they had become fully present and aware and decided to make the right choices for themselves. Why? Because it felt right. In their gut. It felt real to them to trust their gut, by becoming aware of what they were listening to and responding to. The energy in the room went up 100%. The focus in the room was palpable. The synergy was electric. The clarity of thought and intuitive reasoning was undeniable.

What's this got to do with my ability to speak and live my truth?

Everything! When we are here and now, when we become fully present, we possess a clarity of mind – an awareness – that knows no bounds. Creativity flourishes, decision-making speeds up, and you become super highly effective human beings. For me, we become real purpose-driven leaders.

My desire to mindfully live also comes from living on autopilot for far too long. When I was at drama school I lived truthfully on stage, but off stage I lived a double life. Production after production, I would perform *The Merchant of Venice* playing Prince Aragon. Iago in

Othello. I loved playing Iago. I played it quite evilly but also with a sense of deceit and mistrust and uncertainty of who he was, which was clearly appropriate given the time I was doing it. Life imitating art, or is it the other way around?

I think sometimes we create a world for ourselves that we would rather live in, I certainly did. It's almost like when you hear those stories about people who have double lives. I had this life in London, and I had a wife in Northern Ireland. I had created this little existence in London where I saw Richard and went to drama school, and I don't think anyone I knew in London knew anything about my life in Northern Ireland.

I was going through a lot of stuff about my sexuality then, and it's quite peculiar that I didn't think I had an issue with my sexuality while I was at drama school. I convinced myself of the lie. Convinced others of the lie. Our words and deeds are the very nets we throw around ourselves. I used to call Jeanette, we'd chat, and I'd tell her how much I cared for her, but all the while I was having an affair with someone else and had been going out to gay bars and what have you.

One of my big things now is being truthful and removing deceit and anything associated with being anything other than standing in my own true purpose. No autopilot. Mindfully living. Experiencing every moment. What you see is what you get. Even with my relationship with David; it is what it is.

I think it's fascinating that I spent a year on stage learning the craft of acting, and through that being somebody else, I realised who I was. I think everyone should go through that.

So to be able to listen and respond, you need to be present. You need to pay attention. You need to tap into your gut feel. Trust your gut. I have spent the past twenty years developing this approach to life and business. I know when it works and when it doesn't. I understand the power being aware can have on decision-making and business effectiveness. Although recently I heard myself being part of a conversation about awareness becoming an over-used term.

I couldn't quite get my head around this statement. We attach to this base human component of life – paying attention, mindfulness, being present – this horrendous, facile, fashionable perspective. He was saying, *"Isn't it just a fad like everything else in business?"* No! This way of being has been around for centuries. My next line to him was rather wanky. It still is come to think of it, but it's true. I said, *"We are entering an age of wisdom where we want to use the data and information wisely, for a higher purpose."* He responded with, *"So when does one become fully-aware?"*

I don't believe you can become aware and fully present all of the time. I believe it is impossible in normal life and business. We have many differing demands placed on us. We are never going to nail it. It's not about nailing it anyway. It's about continuously practicing it. It's living it. So this thing I help people through is called public speaking. This is merely a vehicle through which you get to grips with your ability to be more aware and thus tap into your gut feel more readily. Then use this freedom and power to make decisions that in turn have profound effects on you and your audience. Paying attention gives you the space to be the real you. It gives you the openness to make the right choices about the right habits for you and your business. For your family. For life. And fucking hell, I discovered it not in Tibet or Goa; I found it in room full of wannabe actors years and years ago.

The Practice: Meditation

Even though I found it on stage with a bunch of actors, I am not suggesting that's how you must find it. You can learn to pay attention from the pages of this book if you apply the practices. One of the most fundamental practices for learning how to pay attention is by developing a regular daily mediation practice.

About four years ago, I found this app on my phone called Buddhify. It has been a life-saver. It is a collection of guided mediations for everyday life. I use it religiously every night before going to sleep and during the day. It is simple to use. I strongly recommend downloading it or one similar and building a practice of daily meditation.

I Am Always Noticing My Emotions

I was a sex-worker. I got paid to have sex with people. Some would call me a prostitute – I was. I got called up for a new job one night, and it was a chap who had a few people over at his place, and he needed someone to come and join the party. So there I was, invited to this party, and I was going to get paid because I got paid for my party attendances. It was actually in a shop. I got to this address, and it was a lighting shop. I then called the person, and they said, "*Yeah, yeah. Just ring the doorbell.*" So I rang the doorbell, and he took me through this lighting shop to this flat, and there were a whole lot of gentlemen taking drugs, and I became their bucket.

I think it's fucking ridiculous when I think about it now. I mean, talk about no sense of self! Fear and self-loathing. Who was I? I didn't know myself. I was unable to see myself. In fact, I completely ignored myself. But I was good at what I did. Can I say that?

I was at rock bottom. People say when you get to rock bottom it's good because the only way is up. Prostitution wasn't quite my bottom (if you pardon the pun). I tried to end it all. That was my real rock bottom. I've always believed when you have seen the bottom there is nothing to fear.

Prostitution was a mistake, a huge fuck up. But with mistakes comes an opportunity to learn and to adjust. It can't be undone. I did it. I made those choices. I continued to develop a profound ability to control my emotions. Much like through the years of abuse. Control with a capital C. Useful in situations such as these, but very unhealthy in life.

When it comes to abuse, there is a violence in every betrayal of trust. My abuse was not only a reprehensible crime of violence against me, the child, but it was against my future as a human being. I became an adult with a disregard for feeling, a disregard for human-ness. Disregard for myself. It wasn't even autopilot behaviour. It was almost like another person. And actually, that other person was that little boy who was sexually abused and had become a man, and whilst that little boy had feelings of being hurt and taken advantage of and feeling dirty and disgusting, there was a sense of control, of mastery that the little boy developed, an ability to manipulate or to manage the situation for himself. And the prostitution was equally the same in that regard.

We make emotional-driven connections because the limbic part of the brain drives our decision making. The limbic brain deals with everything emotional. Our emotional responses to decisions. If we are clear *why* we are speaking, know how we want to show up (be our intent) recognise how this fits with our overall purpose, we can tap into the limbic part of our audience's brain. If we understand our personal, emotional motivation for speaking, and we convey this implicitly in our communication, the audience will connect with us.

How Do You Make the Connection to Your Story?

By recognising the emotion you felt at the time the story took place and allowing yourself to feel a degree of that emotion when you retell that story. In other words, re-live it to tell it. This takes courage and practice. Warning, please make sure you are of sound mind and body before trying this exercise. Seriously, I mean it.

First, you have to be okay with the principle that your feelings and emotions are not yours. I know it's a contradiction. When you can separate *you* from your thoughts, feelings, and emotions, you are on the right track. Secondly, you must cultivate a practice of recognising how thoughts, feelings, and emotions show up in your body. For example, when I am nervous, I feel my shoulders tense up. When I'm upset, I feel a nervousness in my stomach. I have butterflies.

Using a regular mindful practice, notice how you can alter the intensity of the feelings by simply recognising their physical manifestations. You can choose how much you allow them to affect you. Then remember the story in which those feelings, emotions, or thoughts were prevalent. Jot the story down. Have a little black book. Keep a record of the stories. Then when it comes to a talk or a presentation or a meeting where you are required to speak, use a story from your book and identify a relevant emotive-intent, drawing this from within you. Pay attention to what you are experiencing, and what is happening around you.

This practice takes a long time and needs careful consideration and support.

The other day, I was helping a CEO of a global retail

brand get to grips with how he ought to be when presenting to the board. It was an important presentation – Malcolm was about to put forward his ideas for the business over the coming five years. He had worked out what he was going to say. He'd even worked out how he was going to say it. I asked him one simple question: "*How are you going to be?*"

"*I'm going to be me. Deon, don't be ridiculous.*"

I didn't take offense. We'd been working together for a few months now. I re-iterated: "*Give me three emotive words for how you want to conduct yourself when presenting to the board,*"

"*Ahh,*" came the reply. "*I see what you mean. I want to be credible, clear, and on the money.*"

"*That's not three words. What does* on the money *mean in relation to how you will be?*"

"*Knowledgeable.*"

"*Tell me a story from your past where you feel you have either been those three words or you haven't.*"

Malcom told me about a time when he hadn't been those three words and the impact it had on his business. The business failed. He lost the house and his wife left him. I suggested to him this seemingly negative story can be used to highlight how you will *not* be taking the strategy forward as well as how you plan to show up on the day you present it to the board.

He had identified three words that motivated him to speak and lead in a certain way. The thing is, people overcomplicate things. Leadership is seen as an intricate and complex endeavour. It doesn't have to be. If we lead intentionally, and we trust that intention – for that intention is our truth; it is who we are in that moment – then we can cultivate a way of living, a way of leading that is meaningful for us and the people we lead.

But What Intensity of Emotion is Right?

The simple answer is to know your intent. *How do I want to show up on this occasion?* Malcom figured out how he wanted to be. Then he lived it by reliving a degree of emotion from a relevant story.

Your intent has to be all about you. It must be driven by your purpose for life. A by-product thereof. Otherwise, you will come across as an actor hamming it up. You will be inauthentic. You, the leader, playing the role, needs to concern yourself with how you are going to be and trust that this will have the impact you desire.

When you know yourself, be yourself, and trust yourself, you will recognise the level of emotion required. You will listen and respond appropriately. It's that simple. We are not our emotions; they don't own us.

Think of yourself, when speaking, as being on an emotional scale where one is dull, emotionless content delivered with no feeling whatsoever, and ten is being over-the-top, breaking down into tears. Clearly you want to be neither of these two ends of the scale. You will want to play around with this a bit. But go out there and connect with people using your stories, trying out an emotional scale rating of eight perhaps. Or if that's too far for you right now, then how about a seven? Find some guinea pigs and try being emotional. You will begin to recognise your style. Funny thing is, don't look now, but you will be becoming more self-aware – the Holy Grail – if you go out there and try this emotional scale stuff. Notice. But remember, let go of the emotion once you are done. It isn't yours. It isn't you.

We are all emotional beings. We react. We have feelings. People connect to emotion. If they feel something, they are more likely to respond. When we tell stories driven by our own motivational and memorable intent, people feel something; they connect to us and what we are saying.

There is a science behind this emotive-intent malarkey. Storytelling appeals to thought processes and intellect. There's some real scientific basis for my complete belief in the power of storytelling. There are *seven* (yes, seven) areas of your brain that are stimulated by stories. These are the parts of your brain that respond to sounds, smells, language processing of the words that are heard, the comprehension of those words, movement, touch, and finally colours and shapes. So when you talk about what you've seen, heard, felt, or even smelled, your listeners can see, hear, feel, and smell those things too. When you share a story that has meaning for you, they can walk where you have walked. And what could be more effective than that to really convey who you are and what you are really all about? You give your audience a chance to really get inside your heart and your head. That's the connection you need.

Andrew was about to talk to his senior management team. Andrew was so tired of feeling like they didn't understand him. He wanted them to understand why he wanted the business to reach a hundred-million-pound turnover in three years. Telling them hadn't worked. They were with him, so it wasn't as though they didn't have his back. They just didn't seem to get his enthusiasm for growing the business. Andrew decided to identify an emotive-intent for his presentation. He decided to talk to them 'carrying' emotion and holding onto this emotion throughout the time he was speaking to them.

The feedback Andrew received was unprecedented. His colleagues on the team said, *"Andrew, I want to do this with you. I believe we can do it."* But more importantly, Andrew felt that he was living like the leader he knew he was meant to be. Andrew used an emotion which he chose, an appropriate, emotive-intent to drive the way in which he was going to be for the entire time he spoke. He chose the emotion. He decided on the level of intensity. He owned not only the stuff he was talking about, but why he was talking about it and the feelings he wanted others to experience from him.

Start to do away with what you think you should be experiencing, and instead open your heart to what you feel. Listen. And respond. Using your stories from your River of Life will ordinarily make you feel things a little more. They are what you stand for! Connect to what you are saying, and you will be tapping into the right brain of your listeners, the part of the brain that's all about imagination, feeling, creativity, excitement etc. To do this more successfully, more meaningfully, or truthfully, you need to get emotional.

Philip is the managing director of a global technology firm designing apps to change the world. Their signature app is quite remarkable. Can't say any more in here, I'll get into trouble. Philip has been using the same content for quite some time now. In fact, three years. And speaking globally two-three times a month. My work with Philip started by getting him to say his talk to me.

175

He was just going through the motions. Just saying the words. Of course, he also had loads of slides. We got rid of every one of them. The motivation? People wanted to hear him and buy into him, not what he had written on the slides. As soon as the slides were taken away, Philip stood there.

"I can't say what I have always said now."

"Why?" I said curiously.

"Because it doesn't feel right."

"Describe the feeling."

"It feels like I'm just saying words. They don't have any meaning for me. Any feeling."

"But you have said these words before?"

"I think they came from the slides, although they were my words. It feels like I was just reading from the slides. And I know I wasn't."

I got Philip to think of an emotion he wanted to convey

"What? In my presentation for the conference?"

"No, here for me as your audience right now."

Philip chose an emotion and started speaking. His eyes lit up. His physiology changed. He became a lot more animated and didn't use the same words as he had done for the past three years.

With Philip's attention on an emotive word for him, in this case joy, he was able to alter the way he used words and phrases, change his perspective on his presentation and alter the way I (the audience at this time) felt about him and what he was saying.

This has relevance for both livening up talks and presentations as well as making sure you tap into the right-hand side of the brain in your audience. Of course he was still presenting facts and information about his product, but he was now doing it in such a way that made me want to know more at the very least, and at best, I wanted to download the app.

We are emotional beings. We want information. Yes, we do. Data is power. We also want to be stimulated. We want to be able to imagine we are there. Together. Tom Marshall's spiritual and emotional dimensions of intelligence in action. When we have both these elements in our lives, in the presentations or talks we give, in our everyday conversations, we come alive. We buy.

Nowadays, I'm always noticing my emotions in experiences and everyday moments. I no longer seek to control them. They do not control me. I am not the sum of my thoughts and feelings. But I do keep them in a reservoir within me which I draw from when speaking.

Why Do We Stay on the Emotionless Treadmill of Life?

There appears to be an unwillingness to allow ourselves to truly understand our emotions. A fear of using our feelings in conversation with others. Why? Because it's unprofessional? It's shameful to show emotion? Why do we present by numbers? How many talks or board presentations have you done or sat through where you could have just read the slides. Or read an email. The speaker is just going through the motions with no feeling. Why? Fear? Of what? Of being unprofessional? Who defines professional? Fear of being weak? Not at the top of my game? *Look, I can say all these words perfectly and precisely. And I can get to the end of my presentation without making a mistake.*

Don't deny your emotions! Don't let your talks, your engagements, your communications be devoid of emotion. Life is full of ups and downs. Live it. Warts and all. Living your purpose will help you navigate the peaks and troughs. When we push aside normal emotions to embrace false positivity, we lose our capacity to develop habits to deal with the world as it is, not as we wish it to be.

The Practice: Self-Reflection

Each week, I ask myself these questions to help stay true to my purpose and who I know I am. I suggest building a weekly practice of self-reflection using these questions. Add your own as you discover the right questions for you.

1. How do I want to show up this week? Then, before each interaction with someone, I identify an intent and observe myself in action.
2. What emotion have I brought to bear? Which have been useful and in what way?
3. What have I done this week to help me realise my purpose?
4. What am I grateful for this week?
5. What could I do to improve?
6. What have I done well and therefore should do more of?

These questions will help keep you on track, but they will also help you become more aware and able to adjust to situations. Help you respond rather than react.

I have never really been a big forward planner. But I do

swear by the 1-3-5 rule of planning. Use your 1-3-5 plan and these questions to live as fully as possible.

Trust is a Binding Agent and a Lubricant

Religion has played a huge part in my life. Or rather, people's actions and behaviour in the name of religion. I see some of the religious gurus who have crossed my path as being a kind of conversion therapy. They have purported the same version of the same lie: that to be my true self – oh and that includes being gay – is a disease, an error or the result of sexual abuse. That lie created an internal logic for me that carried me down many a destructive path that went on for years. When you believe in the internal logic, you live it.

I lived an unhealthy pattern in my life – a groove of shame I walked, where everything from my body, my sexuality, my relationships, my childhood sexual abuse, went back to a place of disgust, hatred, and self-loathing. Every time I had sex, I would be transported back to Gary's bedroom. This fuelled by the guilt instilled in me by people of the cloth compounded my shameful disease. *"You are not normal, Deon. This is not you. This is not good. This is not good enough. You can be delivered from these chains and made whole. You can step into the light of Christ and be the real you. Let me deliver you from this pain. Denounce your homosexual desires, for they are connected with your abuse."*

This external doctrine became my internal compass. A

compass magnetised by guilt. I remember an almost daily occurrence where a group of church brothers would lay hands on me, praying for the evil spirt of homosexuality to leave my body. I was married at the time. I went along with it. Love the sinner, hate the sin.

I had grown up being fearful of who I was, and who I might become. The possibilities frightened me. I could be anything I put my mind to, so my mother regularly suggested. Little did she know her suggestions fell on deaf ears. I didn't believe her. I seemed to believe *they* might find out about me. This drove an unwillingness to open up and be truthful. It built the foundation for the lies and deceit that would pepper my life until drama school. Then there was the ideology that appeared to be instilled in me by people of the cloth and professionals who were meant to help me. That sexual abuse makes homosexuals. That if you think you're gay, it's only because of the abuse. "*We need to correct this, Deon,*" they would say. *You are right to be homophobic. You feel shame because of this. It is right to feel shame. And the guilt, well, Deon, that's because of your possessed thoughts.*"

I began to believe them. I trusted them. This took on a whole new level when my father some years later after I had decided to come out and be my true self, told me I was possessed by an evil spirit. When this logic forms the backbone of your formative years and of your early adult life, being never good enough becomes your norm. Being shame-ridden set me on a path of shamefulness, self-loathing, self-denial. The horrid thing about all this is that it has happened to so many people and is still happening today.

This makes me think about trust. Go to Amazon and

search for the word 'leadership'. More than 180,000 entries will come up. Some believe that to be a successful leader, they need to find the magical keys, take the right steps, follow the proper laws, figure out the dysfunctions, embrace the challenge, ascend the levels, or discover the ancient wisdom. In other words, overcomplicate things. What if successful leadership isn't really that complicated? What if there is just one thing – not a title, power, or position – that determines whether people follow a leader? Simply just trust.

It's the foundation of any successful, healthy, and thriving relationship. Without it, leadership is doomed. Creativity is stifled, innovation grinds to a halt, and reasoned risk-taking is abandoned. I didn't trust the people in authority. Without trust, your teams check in their hearts and minds at the door, leaving managers with staff who have quit mentally and emotionally but remain on the payroll, sucking precious resources from the organisation. Trust simultaneously acts as the bonding agent that holds everything together and as the lubricant that keeps things moving smoothly. Stephen M.R. Covey, author of *Speed of Trust*, said that while high trust won't necessarily rescue a poor strategy, low trust will almost always derail a good one. What happens if all leadership is, is to have the intention to trust and be trusted?

I got into prostitution. I know it was about wanting to be seen as trustworthy, reliable, dependable. Strange, but true. A desire to want to belong to something, to feel connected to something. A distorted perspective. Let's face it, a disturbingly unhealthy way of seeing the world. Of seeing myself. I had formed habits that created an adult image of myself that was driven by guilt and shame. But the core of my being was not destroyed by my adolescent abuse and the length of time I had to go on to survive it. I was left vulnerable and cold to life. But not any more. The reforming of new habits through conscious choices over the years and the finding, speaking, and living my purpose has changed it.

To act, to lead, to live in this world means we must trust. Trust our own judgement, feelings, and thoughts to make sense of the world. I do this now, of course not 100% of the time. But I trust myself more than ever before. I trust why I am here. I know why I am here. Do you trust in yourself?

Lack of Trust Fuels a Fear of Rejection

I had girlfriends at school. The girlfriend I'll always remember was Zelda. She was stunning. Punching above my weight? Defo! I met her at St John's. We went on a date to the movies with Brendan and his girlfriend. After that, I just didn't call her. It's hilarious and sad. I had no idea how to foster a trusting relationship, let alone a relationship with a girl.

We had an inter-school athletics event with her school, and I bumped into her. She said that it was a good thing it was over. And in my mind, I was being dumped. And that was the first time I'd ever been dumped, and I was distraught. I really didn't understand why she was dumping me even though we hadn't spoken. I was deeply unaware of the mistrust I had fuelled. That rejection stung. But at the same time, this experience also said to me loud and clear, *you know who you are*. I was too afraid to recognise it.

Nobody likes rejection because we want to belong; we want to be liked. We want to be respected. We want to have a sense of value. We want to be seen as trustworthy. Validated. How many times do we fucking check how many likes we have on Facebook? We post things on there because we want to be liked. We want validation. We want people to think we do certain things and live in a certain way.

Trust is a funny thing. We know it has to be built on openness. On honesty and respect. On truth. Our emotional truth.

For far too long, I lived to control my emotions. Manipulating a life of untruths. I built my house on the sand of mistrust, deceit, and down-right lies. Why wouldn't I fear rejection? Anybody who'd lived the same way would too. Respect? Please. The only way up was to live my truth – my purpose. It is the missing link in building trust. And I hadn't lived truthfully for far too long.

Your Primary Objective is to Instil Trust and Confidence That You Will Share the Facts

I've talked a lot about emotion and feelings and bringing these to bear when engaging others. There is room for the *right* data and information too though. The other day I was watching a very renowned and trusted news channel. I was shocked at the blatant misinformation and reporting of an event. What was being reported was an opinion-driven story. Perhaps that's what we crave now. I am all about *my story*, helping people find theirs and tell it. And let's face it, our stories are responses to how *we* have experienced the *actual* course of events. Just opinion. This whole book is about *this* very thing, my interpretation of my life's events.

We want stories. But I believe we also want facts. We want the right data and information, but more importantly, we want to trust. We want to trust ourselves, trust the people we have relationships with, trust politicians and business leaders. We want to believe in the truth. But whose? We find ourselves in a world going through a phase, the loss of trust. There appears to be an unwillingness to believe information, even from those closest to us. The loss of confidence in information channels and sources, and I include social media here, is a tsunami of mistrust.

For you as a leader of people, there are expectations of you. Your primary objective is to instil trust and confidence. In my experience, people want business leaders to take the lead in making the change instead of waiting for government. For example, making the changes in wage imbalances. Don't be clouded by the desire to present hearsay opinion as data and information.

There is a way out of this *fake news* conundrum. Share the right data and information by using emotion and feeling (and your story) to connect with your audience, not delude them.

Facts speak to an audience, but a story wins them over. You reach their hearts and minds. If I try to visualise this in my head, I think about a brain being on a dimmer switch. Facts and figures light up isolated parts of your brain. Using a true story that is unique to you and is driven by an emotive intent allows the light to flood right across the brain.

I was on the tennis court recently – I am always there. I am driven to perfect my Federer backhand, but I am happy with this trial. I love it. I was 4/5 down in the final set. Against an opponent that had always beaten me. I was serving at 30/40. I was one crappy shot away from losing. My body was falling apart, every muscle and sinew was aching. Three hours on a court at my age is a sight to behold. I noticed I had a choice. I could choose to listen to the fear of losing, or breathe, focus, and listen to an emotion I wanted. I chose the latter. I chose an emotive-intent. *Belief.* It energised and focused me. I won the match 5/7, 7/6, 10/8. Epic.

Now you can argue whether or not *belief* is an emotion, but my point is, that word has meaning for me. It motivates in a certain kind of way. To connect mindfully, you must notice your experiences and choose an emotion that compels you to *be* in a certain way. We do it in our everyday on autopilot.

Let's thrash out a good practice guide for applying all this stuff I've banged on about. Use this guide when preparing for any communication scenario. They say preparation is king. Or queen. This is a simple method for preparing for any speaking scenario. Being fully prepared for your talk/presentation or even conversation in a meeting is one of the best ways to manage nerves, help your audience understand you better, and know how you can change things when necessary. It is the fundamental pillar for being the real you.

The Practice: Preparation

As ever, start with identifying your intent. Get clear on the reason/s why you are speaking. This is all about you and must be motivational, memorable, and mine (yours). The question to ask yourself is, how do I want to show up? Try an **emotive-intent**. The question here is, *what emotion do I want to bring to bear that helps me show up the way I want?*

Avoid copious notes or death by PowerPoint. Get a blank sheet of A4 paper and create a spider diagram. In the centre, write your intent and/or your emotive-intent. Circle it.

Identify what you will say. These are your 'titles' for your **core messages**, the nuggets you will talk about. If you are sharing data and information, these should be your headlines for your content. List them in a clockwise direction around the centre circle – your spider legs. My rule of thumb is if you have ten minutes speaking time, you ought to have no more than three core messages. If you have twenty minutes speaking time, no more than five core messages, and if you have forty minutes of speaking time, no more than six core messages.

When delivering your talk/presentation or in your meeting, you need not say these out loud. But this may depend on whether you need to push home your core messages. It may be that your stories are strong enough, so the core messages will come out loud and clear. Sometimes being very explicit about your core messages, especially in a formal presentation/talk situation, can make the audience feel you are preaching/telling them what to do. This can patronise the audience. Remember, your intent should drive what and how you deliver. Under each core message, brainstorm a few **stories** from your River of Life that may bring to life each core message.

Then get clear on what you want your audience to do as a consequence of you speaking – **call to action.** Be sure not to be driven by this. Allow this to happen. Remember, it is very difficult, if not near on impossible, to have much control over your audience. What you are able to affect very significantly is you, your intention, your stories, and core messages. Be true to you. Hold fast to your purpose. To help you, answer this call to action question:

What do I want my audience to think, feel, and/or do because I have spoken to them?

You could start you answer with: *I want my audience to…*

Now practice your talk/presentation out loud. Yes, it

is best reviewed having heard it out loud yourself. Otherwise, you won't know how it sounds and whether what you are saying fits with your intent and resonates with you. If it doesn't do either of these two things, it won't work with your audience either. Remember, you are not saying it out loud to memorise it. It's not a script.

If you do not have the time to go over the whole talk out loud, you can top and tail. Memorise the first sentence and the last sentence. Then if there are a number of core messages, memorise the first and last sentence of each section. This will give you the confidence and freedom to tell stories which will lead you to these opening and closing sentences. If you need to create cue cards, then do so from the 'titles' of your core messages. Or if you insist on using PowerPoint, use one slide per core message, one side for your introduction, and one for your conclusion. Remember, less is more, so be sure to not crowd your slides with too much text.

Reflection Questions/Points:

1. What did you notice when you practiced out loud?
2. What stories could you use from your bank of stories?
3. Did preparing with the use of a spider diagram help? If not, could you approach your written prep in a different way? What way?
4. How many core messages are you wanting to convey?
5. How have you decided to end your talk/presentation? Do you have a strong enough call to action for your audience?

6. Understand intent and call to action are two sides of the same coin. They feed off each other. They must complement each other.

7. Remember *not* to just focus on your call to action. If you do, your talk or presentation will never feel real to you, and you may come across as presenting by numbers, patronising the audience, or worse, direct hard selling.

8. When doing a talk or presentation, have a clear intent that is memorable, motivational, mine – what was the impact? Use feed-forward to review your success in using the power of intent.

9. When using intent to drive your talk, what did you notice about yourself and your audience? Use feed-forward to respond to this question. Ask yourself this question after every talk or presentation.

10. When rehearsing, be curious about your body language, tone of voice, and movement. If you want to walk, walk for a reason, don't shuffle or fiddle. The same applies when you are doing your talk or presentation for real. Do everything for a reason.

Like Everything in Life, You Need Time to Make Some New Memories

When people ask me what I do, I usually tell them I help people become better public speakers. It's such a pants elevator pitch. So dull. You would have thought I'd be good at the elevator. Nah, quite shit as it happens. The public speaking is merely a single outcome of what I do.

What I really do is help people find their story and live and lead with the right intention in each moment. A big part of this is helping them discover new memories that pave the way for them to be excellent. But it doesn't stop there. I get them living their story – presently – every day. Being a truthful, intention-driven leader, speaking their truth in meetings, one-to-ones, board meetings, at the water cooler (if businesses still have such things), and in public speaking scenarios – in every scenario of their life.

There is scientific evidence behind what can help make a great speaker, presenter, communicator, leader. Call it whatever you want. It's great to get some hard evidence for things that I have, in the past, just felt to be true!

Neuroscientists at Oxford have explained that beliefs and memories are very closely linked, and that memories are really formed when 'networks of neurons fire' when they are set in motion by a particular experience or event. So that memory could be one about a great experience you had with a client. On the other hand, it could be a not so good experience you've had when pitching, presenting, or getting the team to follow your new idea. And the more that network of neurons is used – when the neurons fire again and again due to similar experiences – the more the memory is set in stone. It's not hard to see how these memories provide the foundation for your belief system. That's why for me, some of the hardwiring I have had has been, well, let's just say less useful than it could have been. Think, for example, about your memories of pitching and presenting – of speaking in front of an audience. I'm sure most people can recall the times when things haven't gone that well when public speaking. And the more we remember these, the more it affects belief in our own ability. Simples.

I felt like I never had a voice in English class. I was sitting at the kitchen table talking to David and Caroline (a beautiful woman inside and out, and god-mum to William) a little while ago, and we were talking about literature, and in particular, we were talking about *Howard's End*. They had read it as an A-level text, and they were talking about particular themes in it and what it meant. The theme was connecting, and I never would've been able to come up with that at that age. But in their English classes, they were encouraged to share their ideas.

In my English class, I never wanted to put my hand up to share an idea. We sat on particular tables, and there were only two tables that Mr Tennant would discuss things with in class, and I remember feeling that I couldn't contribute ideas or thoughts or feelings about an argument or a judgement of literature.

We had these English and Afrikaans oral exams where we had to prepare a speech, a presentation really. But the funny thing was, I'm not Afrikaans, but I thoroughly enjoyed preparing my Afrikaans presentations. It was probably because there wasn't any internal judgement on my part. When it came to English oral exams, I hated it. I hated public speaking, and I hated standing up presenting because I didn't believe I had a voice. Wasn't good enough.

Shelley was a girl in my English class, and she was an American foreign exchange student from Seattle, Washington. I thought she was absolutely brilliant because she had a voice, she had opinions, and she voiced those opinions. She was an exceptional public speaker. She was fantastic at writing too. I remember being at her house one afternoon doing our homework, and we were supposed to be writing an essay about Charles Dickens's *Hard Times*, and she had finished hers, and I hadn't because I didn't know what to write. I had no idea. We had a discussion, and she helped me get an idea of what I wanted to write about. She read hers, and I was like, *oh my God, this woman is a goddess of writing*. She was someone who had strength, had a presence, had a voice, and had an inner quiet confidence that was amazing.

Like everything in life, you need time to make some new memories. The science goes further to say that new memories, and therefore new beliefs, are created by experiences and our perceptions. It therefore stands to reason that with supportive feedback, sound mentoring, and dedicated practising, you can alter your self-belief and build your confidence in every aspect of leading yourself and others. This book is designed to help you form new memories. My hope is you try. You practice the exercises in here. I know when I have got up and tried, I have been most successful. Not always with the best results or outcome, but with the right intention, to be me. My truth.

The *My Game* formula – (S + V) I = P (strengths plus values multiplied by intuition equals purpose) – when applied consistently, when lived, creates new memories by breaking down long-held habits and behaviours that hold you back. The *My Game* formula generates a disruptive process, and quite deliberately so.

The business of life is the acquisition of memories, and when it comes to the end, that's all we have left. What better way to create memories than by telling stories. By living your purpose, your truth.

When I was younger, I swam every day. I was part of a national swimming club. I think I started swimming when I was three years old. I remember going to my friend Lesley's house after school – obvs not when I was three. We would swim and mess about around the pool. It was Africa. Hot. One year I must have spent every afternoon at Lesley's house. I never did homework. It showed.

I failed nearly every subject. I think at the time we were going through some family troubles. Mum and Dad didn't get on. Mum was working all the hours God sent. Dad, well he was taken up with the church and was never around. I failed every term. Mum grounded me for the last term. I wasn't to go to Lesley's house after school. I wasn't to go anywhere. Straight home. She would call me from work on the hour every hour, every afternoon for three months. Mum said, "*You* will *pass your exams at the end of the year. You* will *go to high school next year.*" I believed her.

It's funny. In grounding me, she gave me a choice. I made a conscious choice to succeed, to achieve something I hadn't for the past nine months. She helped me choose success. I worked my arse off and passed at the end of the year. I can still see myself getting my final report card. I scanned over the grades to the bottom left-hand corner. I knew there would be a statement written there. Either *Required to repeat standard five* or *Promoted to standard six*. It was the latter. A wonderful memory that reminds me I have the ability to influence my destiny.

We all have the capability to achieve if we are willing to consciously choose our path and consciously choose what to place our attention on. What we place our attention on drives our intention for what we do, how we feel, and who we are. We believe. Others believe in us. When it comes to your truth, your purpose, your life, what conscious choices are you making? When you are speaking, where are you placing your attention? On the audience? On the nervous butterfly feeling in your stomach? A very famous author and spiritual guru suggests whatever we place our attention on grows and flourishes.

My father became extremely distant in South Africa. The father-son bond Allan and I had with him in Zimbabwe totally disappeared. He became utterly obsessed with the church. He became so fanatical that he lost his job. He also had a business that went tits-up, so my mother had to go out to work. She was an artist, an extraordinary confectioner, and she used to make amazing cakes in Zimbabwe, but she used to do it as a hobby then. So she went and found a job as a confectioner, and she brought in the money.

Eventually, my parents became quite estranged, and

the atmosphere in the house was dreadful. I never wanted people to come and stay because it was horrible to be around them. The energy was awful. Mother tried to fix it, the *broken home*, by having lovely things in the house, beautiful furniture and stuff. I found a home, acceptance, in Stephen and Gary's house: a love and care and friendship. It wasn't like that in our house. My dad was that fanatical that he gave away the video machine because he believed it brought evil spirits into the house. I mean really!

Whenever I have been faced with difficulty – whether it's the stress of the business failures, knowing what is the best decision for the financial strategy, dealing with my feelings of shame and guilt from either being white South African or indeed the shame and guilt of sexual abuse, to dealing with more ordinary things like the illness of a loved one, exhaustion, or just malignant sadness – I have tried to push it away. I have done this in so many ways, not least of all by burying my head in the sand – not wanting to face my demons – to try to 'solve' it. I must fix it. Everything can be and must be fixed. I used these strategies even though they may have stopped working many years ago. Why?

First, 'solving' it is how I was hardwired. Well, I mean taught. I am a problem solver. Well, have been. This method appeared to work so often in the past that it seemed perfectly legitimate to keep doing it this way. But that wasn't living. That wasn't *being*. We've all used the same tactics time and time again in business when we shouldn't. That old saying…*and expecting a different result.*

Second, there is an element of denial; I simply did not

want to admit that I was helpless and vulnerable because I feared others would think of me as not good enough. Not good enough to run a multimillion-pound business. Not good enough to stand up in front of hundreds of people and tell my story. Not good enough to write this book. And deep down, I sometimes think this means I will lose face. So, I have to grind on and on.

When my parents were going through a shit time, I used to say to myself, *they're going to get divorced, but it's nothing to do with me, nothing to do with me.* But it affected me a lot more than I led myself to believe. I think it affected me a great deal in terms of the type of relationships I had. I was very cagey, detached, and unaccepting.

They were going through this hard time, and there were always arguments in the house. I remember hearing them argue once, and my dad told my mother she had to give him her money so he could give it to the church. My mother always wanted to support my dad, but at this point, there was no food in the house. There were only these very shitty processed packs of ten mini pizzas.

I still remember these packs of pizza. They used to have little plastic clips that you could twist to open and close the packet. The pizza would take five minutes to cook. I'd sit watching American sitcoms I wasn't allowed to watch, and I'd eat my rubber pizza. Allan used to microwave them. Rank. Titch, our Fox Terrier, fucking loved them. That's why she got so fat.

I remember exactly what the fridge looked like, and it said something to me: that charity begins at home. It's really stuck with me.

There was this packet of pizzas and powdered milk, which was disgusting. I never drank it. Allan used to drink pint glasses full. I would have it on cereal, but that was the only way I could stomach it.

Allan used to love the pizza too. He would eat them all the time. I didn't. I'd come home from school, and there'd be nothing to eat. That's why I used to go round to Lesley's house after school. I also wanted to go round to his house to fuck around. I wasn't going just to have food, but there was a part of that.

I hated bringing friends home, not only because my parents would argue and there was this atmosphere in the house, but there wouldn't be anything for them to eat. I would go to other friends' houses, and I'd stay over, and there'd be delicious breakfasts made, and Mum and Dad would be there, and it was this ideal family life.

I made a pact with myself that the fridge would always have stuff in it. The freezer too. Oh and by the way it can't be an ordinary fridge either. It has to be a huge fuck-off double fridge. It gave me a sense of real determination and perseverance. I would ensure there was food on the table for my family.

When I discovered the real me, my truth, my purpose and I realised my story too, these old strategies no longer worked. But it was more than that, they became irrelevant, nonsensical. I reached a fork in the road, and I took the one less travelled. But don't get me wrong, it's not as though there has been only one moment and I am sorted for life. I have had these *fork* moments often. A lot during my forty-seven years on this planet.

When I have carried on and pretended there is nothing wrong, I have led an increasingly miserable existence. The light is finding, speaking, and living my purpose. Recognising I am doing this moment to moment in every

200

day, each week, month, and year. This way, this approach to living and leading, is one of acceptance of our true selves and of whatever is troubling us. For me, it has meant turning towards the abuse, rape, business failures, guilt, shame, stealing, prostitution, and drug abuse, and realising the reason for befriending it, even when – indeed, especially when – I haven't liked it, or it scared me. I have accepted these things, and through meditation and daily practice of mindfulness (remember it's simply paying attention), I have created new memories.

Not everyone will understand the path I've taken. I've realised that's okay. I am here to live my life, lead my way, not make everyone understand.

Acceptance for me was a big thing. In fact, it was like heresy of the first order. Acceptance is not resignation. It is not passive. My acceptance of my story (including the intolerable bits, and as you can tell, there are many of those) is not a spineless resignation. It is not giving up. It is a mindful detachment that allows me to use the emotion and feeling I choose when speaking to convey a message and connect with the thoughts and feelings of others. To motivate them to think, feel, or be.

There is a brilliant principle in improv which is called accepting all offers. As an improviser, you must accept what is offered (either by self or others you are playing with) and build on it. This approach to communicating is a *yes...and* mind set and way of being. It fuels your ability to genuinely listen and respond.

With acceptance, we are less likely to have a knee-jerk reaction. Acceptance has allowed me to be fully aware of difficulties, with all the painful nuances, and to respond to them in the most skilful way possible. It has given me more time and space to respond rather than react. It is not passive. It is actively creating new memories.

I Noticed How in Tune I Was

Any decision that I've made in the past and I make now, I make without the desire to rationalise. In fact, when I rationalise, I change my mind and tend not to pick the best option. It was the same when I was swimming. At swimming, butterfly was my weakest stroke. I remember my mother and Mrs Palmer having a conversation, and Mrs Palmer said, *"Don't worry, Jeanne. It'll click one day, and he'll just get it."* And she was right. There was a moment when I was messing around in the pool, and I remember Mrs Palmer screaming across to my mother, *"Jeanne, he's got it! Look!"* And I think that says something about intuition and feeling and doing.

It's the same with baking and cooking. If I think too much about what I'm doing, what I end up doing is not paying attention to what I'm experiencing, and I fuck it up. And yet everything in life in terms of schooling is based on your cognitive ability to reason.

My earliest memory from childhood was my brother, Allan, and I playing in mud at the bottom of the garden. The houses had just been built, and there was no gate. It was 1975, and there we were in the mud. We made mud cakes. In fact, I remember creating a birthday party for my dog, Titch. I made some cake-concoction. No-one in the family wanted to come to the dog's *birthday party* at the bottom of the garden near her kennel. I always wanted to pretend I was baking.

Fast forward to now, I love baking. I guess it's creative and methodical. But most important of all, it is an instinctive process. I love to be left alone in the kitchen with Pink (the singer) blaring, and me singing – obviously off key – at the top of my voice, baking. Christ, even when I'm baking I am performing. Baking allows me the freedom to play. I hardly ever follow a recipe to the letter, always adding ingredients. I do intuitively. It's the improviser in me.

Intuition is defined as the ability to understand something instinctively. Awareness is defined as mastering your intuition in life. In public speaking, in presenting, in communicating with others, it is bringing about conscious awareness. Your intuition, and your ability use your gut feeling to take notice, is the ability to perceive. Your ability to interpret data you are receiving from within you as well as externally and using the feeling this conjures up to take action.

This reminds me of playing tennis, well, at least my perception of it. My tennis coach would say, "*Watch yourself and do what you know to be right to make the shot.*" I would say to him, "*That's fine, but I must know the basics, mustn't I?*"

"*Even people who haven't picked up a tennis racquet before know what to do instinctively,*" he would tell me. "*It goes wrong, Deon, because we tell ourselves* (or we've been told or both) *what isn't right when it comes to making a shot.*"

There is a far more natural way to learn or realise your potential than to be told what not to do or equally what you must do. It's like the process we used when learning to walk and talk as babies. We used our intuitive capabilities driven by our right and left brain. As adults, as leaders, all we need to do is unlearn the habits which interfere with this and just let it happen.

This summer when I was in a doubles match, I was playing on the forehand side, the right-hand side of the court (for those of you not as obsessed with the game as I). I never play on this side, so I guess I was more aware of things. I noticed how in tune I was to watching and hitting the ball. I would go so far as saying I was totes in the zone. I was able to see myself hit the ball with precision. And in that moment, I noticed my surroundings and was able to guide the ball down the line for a winner. Game, set, and match. Well, not quite because it was one set all. But it was game, set, match for me insofar as I realised afterwards I was tapping into my gut – my intuition to play the shot. In this instance, before any thought had come into my mind, my body had reacted. I moved my feet and body into the right position. I kept my head down and finished the shot with my head down (tennis players, you all know the perils of lifting your head mid stroke).

Afterwards, I remembered I had done this a good few times before. I had created a somatic marker. And I was aware of it. I had paid attention. I had created another memory which was being stored in my brain. Now I know we all have various kinds of memory which are stored throughout our brains so we can remember how to use certain skills (even something as mundane as knowing how hard to wipe the loo roll or not) and know how to react to certain situations. Each time we learn or experience something new, the neurons make connections which reflect that experience and release chemicals which trigger particular feelings. This is a somatic marker.

Using your intuition to drive your choices when you present or lead is the Holy Grail.

Have You Ever Had That Gut Feeling?

I'm not talking about the onset of tummy bugs here! I'm talking about that feeling we get when we just 'know' or sense the best course of action, or what's going to happen next. When it comes to business, just like your personal life, your gut has the answers. You might just seem to know when the deal is going to be clinched, or you can see when your best laid plans are about to go a bit pear-shaped. And you can feel it when your talk or presentation needs to be stepped up a notch or changed in some way. But do we always trust our gut? In my experience many people don't.

This thinking takes me back to the 1980s. I was outside at my mate's house, swimming. I must have been about fifteen then. There were about four us messing about... typing this, I can feel the nervous butterflies in my gut and the adrenaline coursing through my body. Just as a side, being present allows me to use this energy to focus my attention on my intention. I could easily have thoughts that do not serve me. Thoughts that cast doubt in this moment about the use of this story. I have had countless hours of therapy on this matter, and I have shared this story when public speaking, so I am totally okay with talking about it.

We were playing a game called Marco-Polo. One

person is on and keeps their eyes shut. He shouts "*Marco?*" The others shout in response "*Polo!*" The intention of the game is for the person who is 'on' to catch the others. It's fun when you're fifteen and in a pool in thirty-three-degree centigrade heat.

There I was, oblivious to what was going on indoors, what was about to happen to me. I guess you could say I wasn't totally present. I began to notice the other boys one by one leaving the pool and then coming back. Andrew came back very red-faced. At first, I didn't care too much about it. I thought nothing of it. Perhaps he'd just run to the corner shop. He did have a bag of crisps in his hand.

Stephen yelled at me, "*Deon! My dad's calling you.*" You know when you know. Gut feel. Intuition. Something wasn't quite what it seemed.

Stephen smiled and did that sideways upward nod with his head, encouraging me to hurry up. I got out of the pool. The sun was really hot. It must have been just past noon. I really hadn't a clue. I hauled myself out of the water. Why did I always do that at the deep-end? Like some Adonis hauling himself out of a pool of water on some swimwear advert. Not.

The slasto under my feet was so hot now. I bet you could fry an egg on it. Or so I thought. I walked quickly to the back door, past the car porch, the car I drove into a tree. The back door was open. Ahh, the cool tiles of the kitchen floor. All I could hear was the bird-like buzzing sound of the ceiling fan interspersed with Elton John. I fucking hate Elton John's music. No offence to the guy, but it just brings me back to *this* house.

Breathe. I do. I take in a deep breath and let it out. I wonder what he wants? What the fuck is going on?

207

Have you ever seen a horror movie where you shout at the television? *No! Don't go down there. Don't.* There's this pause. Pure silence. Stillness. And the character takes a step. The music is chilling in the background.

I pushed the door of Gary's bedroom open. I was, I guess you were too, expecting it to creak just like in the movies. It didn't.

He was lying on his bed with the bedsheets pulled down. A sight and a pattern that was to be repeated for far too many years. The curtains were drawn. There was a light coming in from the dressing room area. He looked up. Smiled. Playing with his hard cock. What the? "*Come,*" he said. I must have stood there for days. It felt like forever. "*Come on, come. Close the door.*" I stepped in. And closed the door behind me. I didn't even turn around to close it. I was fixated. What the fuck!

Pause! Rewind. Pause and rewind this film of my life. Now, press play and this time don't turn right. My *sliding doors* moment. For the first time in years, I didn't. No. I didn't turn right into the passage and walk down to Gary's bedroom. I took a breath, a moment.

"*You know what to do here, Deon.*"

I turned left, and I went into the living room, picked up the phone, and called my mother. It was instinctive. I said, "*Mum, come and get me.*" She asked me why, and I said, "*Just come and get me now.*" I didn't explain, and I didn't say anything to Gary when my mum's car pulled up except that my mum was coming to fetch me. He asked me why and asked me what was the matter, but I didn't tell him. He brought my mother into the living room and made her a cup of tea and everything. And I remember sitting there, and that man had done what he'd done for so many years, but I couldn't say anything. But thankfully my mum came, and I went home with her.

We all need to learn to trust our gut feelings. But don't just take my word for it. Those brainy scientists say it's actually the foundation of rational decision-making. I know that some people are quite convinced that emotion and reason are in conflict with each other. Ever heard your friends or family members wail, *"Oh, I wish I had listened to my head instead of my heart?"* I know I've said that in the past. Now I don't. Scientific research shows that emotion and reason are very much intertwined. To make good decisions, you actually need to have completed some type of emotional processing before the reasoning part of the process can be effective.

To put it another way, when you're speaking in public or presenting, you need to feel something first in order to make a sound, rational decision to change what you're saying. Or how you're saying it. And when you do feel this, when you've done this 'emotional processing' as it's called, then this will help to speed up your 'on the spot' decision-making. You'll then be far more able to step up your presentation a notch or two.

Somatic markers are those gut feelings, or hunches (or whatever you want to call them). When you're anxious, what do you feel? Maybe a bit tense or even a bit sick in the tummy? And maybe when you're more content, your whole body feels differently. I know for me that my shoulders just feel differently. So when you're standing up there speaking and making a call about the audience's level of engagement with you, these physical sensations can guide you towards making changes in your approach. Hence the belly-breathing exercise.

Let's take an example. Imagine you're speaking to a large audience of business owners for the first time. You see about two hundred people looking at you. That's four hundred eyes bearing down on you. That's exciting for some, perhaps a bit scary for others. What's actually going on in your brain at this point? Well, it's working overtime. It's trying to make predictions using non-cognitive information from the outside world – your previous experiences from former speaking gigs and presentations (which may or may not have been good) and internal emotional information (the fear, comfort, or exhilaration you feel in response). This combination of information then gets served up to you in a physical sensation. That's the feeling in your gut. When presenting, if you practise noticing these sensations and physical signs, you can use them in a positive way to make good, useful decisions about what you're saying and how you're saying it. Make new memories.

Making your presentations, talks, or even your everyday communications driven by this level of intuition will make you deliver your messages and story more appropriately for different and particular audiences.

In sport, intuition is often key. When I started swimming competitively in Zimbabwe, Mrs Palmer said I could be an exceptional swimmer if I just trusted my gut and swam with belief. She told my mother I could be better than Allan, and that was a huge thing for me. We were two years apart and in constant competition.

That day I was beaten in the hundred fly by a hundredth of second, the day I let Mr Doubt creep in, was a moment I didn't trust my gut. I didn't allow myself to just let it happen. I let *Self 1* take control. Trust your intuition. It's been with you since birth. Use it.

How Do I Use My Gut Feelings?

In my experience, the belly-breathing exercise is key. It's all about cultivating a practice of mindfulness, paying attention. Once you have mastered belly-breathing, you will be able to pay attention to the feelings and sensations in your body in any situation. When you can do this, you will be better equipped to trust those feelings and sensations and complete the *emotional processing* and make good decisions.

I Love Being the Director

You need to cultivate a sense of freedom, an open-mindedness, and a willingness to discover the possibilities of doing things differently. You need to trust the influential capability in your story. You need to go emotionally to places you may well have never gone before. As I have said, when you connect with your history and use it well, others follow you. Flexing your style of leadership but remaining true to you is crucial to building trust. Knowing who *you* truly are and using this power in service of others is the real truth of leadership. This is about being the real you. The authentic you. I know that word is used a lot nowadays.

You have to find, speak, and live your truth. This is about being curious about yourself and giving yourself the freedom to speak it. You *can* be the one people remember. You will be the one who grows from being a great leader to an exceptional leader. You will walk into a room, and the energy will rise. People will notice you. They will wait in anticipation for what you might say. Not because of your position or title, but because of you.

Recently, in fact last year, I was brought in to host an event at a global corporate financial services firm for thirty women who were recognised as amazing leaders. The HR director brought me in, and he wanted me to meet them before the event.

The event organiser who led me up to them sort of crept up to the door, much like a child would do when they're sneaking about, she was very submissive about it. She opened the door and sort of went, "*Could I, maybe I could just, would it be all right if...*" I thought, *what the fuck? These are just human beings.*

The HR director was very strict about what I was supposed to do. He wanted me to talk to them for three minutes and told me I needed to be very specific about what I was going to say and introduce the evening and how it was going to flow. Even he felt as though he had to act in a particular way.

Eventually, I was brought in, and I was just me. I said hello, and I asked them how they were. Some of them said fine, and others mumbled, as you can imagine. "*Hello?*" I said. "*Hang on a minute. I asked you a question.*" Delivered in a very camp, playful way, with an outrageous flirtatious lilt to boot.

The HR director started to nudge me and said, "*Deon's just going to—*"

I interrupted him and said, "*Let me.*" He had this strange desire to behave in a peculiar, almost submissive fashion which was constrained and formulaic and inhuman, like these people were gods. But they were just people. Be in the moment and be yourself, and if they don't like you, fuck 'em.

I got them on side, and some of them came up to me afterwards and told me how refreshing it was to have fun and just be. But I was only me. Just myself. I see everything as an adventure. I saw going into that room as an adventure because it's a blank canvas. I didn't know how they were going to react. I didn't know exactly what I was going to say or how I was going to say it. And that excited me. Pure improv.

If I had gone in there and just said the things I needed to say, I would never have had the opportunity to be myself and interact with them because none of that would've happened. And they did more as a consequence of me being that way, of me being myself. Why can't business be more like that?

I argue that we should strive to move from a state where we just randomly respond to things emotionally, to a state where we are able to respond with propriety. Developing propriety does not mean overcoming or controlling the emotions. Feeling emotion is what makes us human. It simply means cultivating our emotions so that we find better ways of responding to others. We choose appropriate, relevant emotions depending on our intent.

I have spent a lifetime letting go of control. When I was about fifteen, I was obsessed with calligraphy. Aunty Joan, my mother's twin, was phenomenal at it. Some of her work looked like medieval scroll writing. You know the kind that you'd expect monks of the cloth to be sitting at for hours and days on end.

Gary used to buy me calligraphy pens and want me to come over and do stuff for Stephen's projects and things. And then he would fuck me. Afterwards, I would get out of the bedroom and go to the shower to wash myself, and I would bawl my eyes out. Clinging to my ritual routine to keep guilt and shame at bay. Over time, I got used to it, and I wouldn't do the crying any more. I developed an unshakable ability to control the situation, including my thoughts and feelings.

We can start to respond to people in ways that we have

cultivated instead of through immediate emotional reaction, refined through rituals. Our habits. Most of us have certain rituals without even noticing. A morning cup of coffee, family dinners, a couple's regular Friday date night, or a piggy back ride for the kids at bedtime. We consider these moments important because they give our lives continuity and meaning and bond us to our loved ones. Confucius says that these moments are potential rituals that teach us about who we are. Consider a simple fact that we all engage with others multiple times a day.

We run into a friend and we say, *"Hey, how's it going? Great, how about you?"* The bare facts connect you for a moment before you continue. In conversations such as these, I long to say sawubona, I see you, but it just doesn't feel right. Then he/she introduces you to someone else. You greet them and all make breezy chitchat about the weather (if you're in the UK), the surroundings, or some recent news events.

You run into a close friend at the supermarket. You stop your carts and give each other a warm hug. *"How have you been? The kids are great."* You have a short, animated conversation and promise to make a date for coffee before you go your separate ways. It's perfunctory. It isn't present-moment-ness.

On these occasions, we use different greetings and different sorts of questions and use different tones of voice when talking to different people. All of this we do subconsciously. We adjust our behaviour and the very words we use depending on whether we are talking to a close friend, acquaintance, someone we just met, our mother or father, boss, coach, or your child's piano teacher.

We modify the way we speak according to who we are

with because we have learnt this is the socially appropriate thing to do. It's the role you've been told to play. What about the role you know you ought to play? And because we are with different people in different situations all day long, everything we do shifts constantly. Equally, we do this at work. Over time, surely we begin to question who am I then? If who I am being is constantly and consistently driven by what I believe is socially acceptable, then what is the real me? And we do this in the office, right? We accept it because it's called culture. The way things are done around here. Why can't you be the one that stands out from the crowd? The one that is remembered. The one that sets the culture?

I'll never forget when Emma and I were in Bristol in the head office of an engineering firm. The company was populated with men, and there was one woman in amongst nine men. We were working with the senior executives there. Every time Emma asked a question or challenged one of the men to do something, they would direct their response to me. Emma called them up on it.

But what struck me was that this woman did the same. In business, a lot of leaders feel as though they must behave in a certain way to fit in. Christ, I know I have done similar. They must adopt certain rituals. They think that to be successful, they must *act* as other successful people do. And because of that, this woman believed she had to develop the 'male' attributes her colleagues had for her to be successful.

I asked her, "*Why don't you just be yourself? Why not show the relevant emotion I sense you want to show? What is stopping you from just being you?*" And this was when I realised I loved helping people become more aware. I loved helping people pay more attention to what they're doing. I loved being the *theatre* or *film director* and them the *actors* playing different roles.

She didn't even notice she was doing it. She had no idea. She was absorbing the behaviours of those around her. She thought success was being someone she wasn't. There was a moment she was about to break down, and I could see she was going to stop herself, and I told her not to.

Sometimes I Just Want to Be Outrageous

Sometimes on Saturdays, I go to football with William and I stand on the side line with the other dads. There's one dad that I know, Dan, and we chat, and because we know each other, we get over the 'hi how are you' business quite quickly, and we can move onto something more significant.

A little while ago, there were a couple of other dads there, and I find it funny because I've seen Emma in those situations, and she has a lot in common with them. They all love football, and they watch football. Whereas I know fuck all about football. Well, I know it's a round ball.

And so I was standing there, and Dan introduced me to the other two dads, and they were talking about 'the wife'. You know how men do that; they talk about 'the wife' or 'the missus', whatever. They were talking about their wives giving them permission to watch more football on TV, and they were saying it in the context of making their monthly premiums worthwhile, so they needed to watch it a lot more. Yeah. Sure. So of course, I pipe up and say we don't do that, and I explained the series of apps we use. And they were all fascinated by it, and then one dad said, "*Well, your missus must be really happy.*" So I replied, "*Well, I don't have a missus.*" And there was silence. Dan said, "*Go on then. Tell them. Tell them. Let them know.*"

I mean, are they blind? Do they not see the rainbow flag hanging out of my arse?

So of course, they're quite keen to find out. And sometimes I say outrageous things because it's fun. I want to be Gina String. So I said the rudest thing I could've said in that context. I said, "*I take it up the shitter.*" My Julian Clarey moment. Who says that? My heart was pounding in my chest. Tumbleweed. They absolutely and utterly didn't know what to do. I interjected, "*Just kidding.*" Breaking the ice.

Dan went, "*No, you're not.*" And then belly laughter ensued. But I mean, why didn't I just say, "*I'm in a gay relationship*"? Why couldn't I just say that? It's like I've got to go and stand up in front of the whole school in suspenders and a bra. Why can't I just melt away into the crowd? But it's fun. The intent is playful married with a little bit of shock and awe.

So then they wanted to know all the ins and outs about Emma and us and whatnot. How it works and what happens. "*So you're together?*", "*No, we're not together.*" And then we got talking about sport and tennis. What was great about it was that they invited me to play tennis at their club. And what I mean by 'great' is that even though I was being outrageous, they got to know me, and we didn't have to have those boring, introductory, perfunctory conversations. Conversations with a silver lining.

I think that's why I want to go and climb a mountain. Seriously, I do. As well as that, there's a desire to want to experience more than the day-to-day grind. Or maybe it's the age thing. Forty-something mid-life crisis. Perhaps I should climb a mountain as Gina String, AKA *Priscilla Queen of the Desert*. A cock in a frock on a rock.

The Practice: Be More Banana

There is a time and place to be remarkable. And don't get me wrong, I would love to be someone remarkable.

But I believe there is a need to be outrageous at times. So here is my challenge to you (and to me, too): go and do something outrageous once a week. If not once a week, at least once a month. You must do something out of the ordinary for you. Be silly. Be playful. Have fun. Have a laugh. It could be as simple as going to see a bit of comedy at the West End. Do it. Be the child in you again for a moment.

Emma calls it be more banana.

Caught in a *Fantasy* of Freedom and Missing the *Actuality* of Freedom Available

Moving back to South Africa at the age of 11 was a big change for me. It was a huge change for my father, and a huge change for the whole family. When we moved, it was the early-80s. Zimbabwe's war for independence was just over and people used to travel only in convoy. We were travelling to the border, and I remember hearing my parents arguing. They wouldn't row a lot, but when they did, the whole world knew about it. My mother said to my father, "*Why didn't you take that job?*", and I later realised she was referring to a job in Sydney, Australia. She always used to go on about how she never wanted to live in South Africa. She wanted to go to Australia, and we didn't. The move to South Africa tore our family apart.

We arrived in South Africa with twenty-nine rand each, the equivalent of about a fiver each. We had old furniture coming in trucks because you weren't allowed to take out new furniture. Government officials used to come to your house and assess your furniture. If you couldn't prove it was older than four years old, they would take it. You weren't allowed to take appliances out like fridge-freezers and things like that. You weren't allowed to take them out at all.

We stayed in a caravan park. Horrendous. We arrived

late at night. It was the twenty-first of June, so it was the middle of winter in South Africa, and it was freezing cold. Certainly to me, having never experienced temperatures lower than twenty degrees. We got into the caravan, and there was sick on the bunk beds that Allan and I had to sleep on. We went from this idyllic, colonial-style house and farm to living in a caravan with sick on the bunk beds. Mother cried herself to sleep that night.

My mother had to get us into schools, and she got me into a school called Impala Park Primary, and I fucking hated it. I was a fish out of water. As an adult now, I know why. I love change, but I fucking hate it. It frightens me to death, but I'll jump in with both feet, and then I go, *oh my God why didn't I do that sooner?* I didn't know that about myself then. I was lost in sea of a different country, a different home.

In my school in Zimbabwe, we didn't move around class, but now I had to move around class, and I found that extremely difficult. I also found it really difficult to make friends. I had already been to four different schools whilst my dad was looking for a job in South Africa. We stayed with my aunt on the farm, and I went to three different schools in six months, so I felt really isolated and alone. Too much change can be a bad thing.

Because I was battling with my grades, my parents put me back a year, and that had a big implication on the way I felt about myself and my ability to achieve academically and to achieve in general, the *I'm not good enough* scenario playing out once more.

We were there in the caravan park for three months, and then we moved to the other side of Boksburg, which meant I had to move schools again, and that's when I started to kick off.

I remember being in the sick bay with my mother and the headmaster, and I was screaming. "*I don't want to go to school! I don't want to go to class!*" My mother was crying, and I was screaming, and the headmaster came over to me and said, "*Look what you've done to your mother. Sort yourself out. Go to class. Look at the state you've put your mother in.*" But I didn't want to go. I didn't feel like I fit it in.

I have often in my life behaved as though I am tugging on the rope of life just barely and sometimes holding on with a vice-like grip. When things haven't been working out as I'd have liked them to, I have tried harder and kept pushing and pulling in the same direction I wanted to go. I still do it at times. But I notice it now. I am more able to *let it happen* as opposed to always trying to *make it happen*. I know it is not always sensible to keep relentlessly pushing in one direction. The noticing now allows me to pause before simply waiting for things to pan out as they might, spotting opportunities as they arise.

Zimbabwe was just the perfect upbringing. We had a huge house, Richard, our gardener, and Emily, our maid who I loved and adored. They were an amazing couple. I recently found out they were married for sixty years. We had a pool, and we used to go swimming, and we went to friends' houses, and it always felt like there was no parental guidance or anything like that. It was just freedom. I saw Zimbabwe as complete freedom. My mother never worked, and we had this beautiful close-knit family. White privilege though.

In 1981, we went as a family on a train trip to South Africa. This is a lasting memory I have of the good times in the family. We went down to Cape Town from

Bulawayo in Zimbabwe. It was three days on the train. It was an utterly amazing experience. My dad would wake us up at five o'clock in the morning and take us right to the front of the train while it was going through the semi-desert area, the Karoo. There were snow caps on the mountains just outside this town called De Aar, and I had never seen snow. The sun was coming up, and we would sit there while he told us stories. The dry, red sand smell of Africa would waft through the open window and we were just enthralled. It was an amazing trip.

Zimbabwe was kind of an adventure too. We spent a lot of our time being mischievous. For example, the gates at the end of the driveways could be lifted off the poles they were on in the ground, and we used to go down the road just before nightfall and lift Mr Fitzsimons's gates off and take them right down to the end of the street where there was this huge ditch, and we'd just bung them in the ditch. That's the sort of mischief we used to get up to as kids. How ridiculously colonial is that?

As a child, I approached life as most children do, with curiosity, wonder, and sense of experiencing things for the first time. When I have done stuff with negative or critical mind set, much like my days as a prostitute or if I have been overthinking or worrying about the outcome, or even completed a task with gritted teeth I have activated my mind's aversion system. This has narrowed the focus of my life and choices. No wonder or inquisitiveness. When I have done exactly the same thing in an open-hearted, welcoming manner, I have activated my mind's approach system, and then my life has a chance to become richer, warmer, more flexible and more creative. This is why finding, speaking, and living your truth is crucial for a healthier you. It has been for me.

When I felt trapped in my marriage by my desire to deny the truth about my sexuality, I felt exhausted and helpless. Exhausted by not only living a lie, but helpless to know what to do about it. I was trapped by my own sense of duty – a marriage is for life no matter the consequences. I was trapped by sense of responsibility. Much like I was trapped in a cycle of business failures because of my inability to pause, to notice. I know this came from the past when I have felt I had to prove something to myself or to others. That neediness. And over the years, this has turned into a script that has kept me locked in old habits. Un-serving rituals.

The 'self-attacking' aspect of me has brought me to the very horrid things I have mentioned in here: drugs, stealing, prostitution, deceit, and lies. The simple act of turning towards my negative spirals and observing them has helped to dissolve such patterns. I was caught in a *fantasy* of freedom and missing the *actuality* of freedom available to me.

At school in Zimbabwe, they used to stream the classes: A, B, and C. At the beginning of the year, you all had to line up in assembly, and your name got called in front of everybody, and you had to go and stand in your new class. One year my name got called for the A class. I did a double take – come again! I almost strutted over, feeling amazing about myself, walking like John Wayne. I certainly felt like the cat that got the cream.

The next day, Mr Ian Morrison Young, the headmaster, with his Hercule Poirot moustache came and knocked on the door of the classroom I was in. He wanted a word with me, so I left the classroom, and he told me there and then that I was in the wrong class. He told the teacher I was in the wrong class and I had to get my bags and go with him to the B class. All that did was tell me I wasn't good enough. And that's followed me round: *you're not good enough*. I was nine.

But here's the crucial piece…take responsibility. Practising is key. You have to be willing to take action to change both the thoughts and feelings that are not serving you. This takes a lot of practising. To be a master at this, you'll need to develop an acute awareness of your emotional responses and decision-making in experiences or situations and be able to distinguish between the ones that serve you and are useful, and the ones that are not. You need to create the actuality of freedom. You know you need to do this and take action and be the formidable presenter, public speaker, leader and indeed person that you can most certainly be. If I can do it, and now teach it, so can you.

In order to trust your gut, to tap into your intuition, you need to start paying attention. When we pay attention, i.e. become aware, whole cascades of chemicals fire into action. Every nanosecond we shift our attention, our brain has a complete makeover and changes shape; our minds are in continual flux and shaping into another form.

Christopher is a CEO and a good speaker. At a recent talk in Helsinki, there was a Q&A session after his talk. He remembers standing up there having really strong feelings of anxiousness. Thoughts that he may not be able to respond to a question well enough. An anxiousness that he might not have the answer or just clam-up in fear. He felt like he had been singled out. Good enough to be there, but not good enough to have the answer. "*I fear that they may find out I don't know. I don't have the knowledge. What would that say to the audience? What would that say to me? What would that say about my capability and my leadership? What does that say to me and the audience about my ability when they look up to me?*"

In this scenario, Christopher wasn't able to separate emotional responses in a situation from real, useful thoughts. He is able in other circumstances. I got him to do the *Circle of Perspective* practice. He also realised in that moment that our practice of belly-breathing and learning to place his attention on this physical act allowed him to let go of the emotional responses, distinguishing these from thoughts that would help him communicate effectively with the audience. Whilst in the moment of doing this, he was able to be present in the moment and respond to the questions.

Christopher and I had spent some time in one-to-one sessions helping him master this craft, but he too had spent time applying the practice. A tricky practice that never ends. I went to watch his latest talk, and Christopher's sense of ease was palpable. His command of the talk and Q&A and his ability to respond in the moment fuelled a sense of confidence he had never felt before.

This exercise can be used to help you master any aspect of leadership, speaking, or of self you feel less confident with.

The Practice: Circle of Perspective

You are going to draw a spider-diagram or mind-map.

Get a sheet of paper. A4 size will do. In the middle,

draw a circle and write the word *confidence*, or it could be *leadership* or *presence* if you think you a battling with mastering either one of those. Essentially, the word that describes what you want to develop. Now draw at least half a dozen legs for your spider.

Exploring *confidence* as an example, I asked Christopher to think about a person he knew that he believed was confident. I asked him to close his eyes and picture them. We were in a private room, so he didn't feel like a knob. I then asked him, "*What are the traits or attributes they possess that makes you believe they are confident? Write down those attributes on the sheet of paper, one trait for each of the six spider legs.*" He wrote down stuff like *voice, body language, knowledge, decision-making, presence, speaking.*

I then asked him to rate *himself* on a scale of one to ten, where ten is high, for each one of those attributes when he was at home and at work. So each spider leg had an *attribute* label and had two ratings out of ten. What he noticed, for example, was on voice he rated himself at a nine at home and only a four at work. There were other variations too.

The question to ask yourself when you get to this point is, how can I translate the skill and ability I have from those high-rated aspects into the lower rated aspects?

My answer: through observation. Noticing when you are thinking un-useful thoughts and replacing them with more useful, confident thoughts that you recognise you have either at home or at work or vice versa.

For Christopher, the exercise helped translate the nebulous concept of confidence into something more tangible. And as I said earlier on, and as I said to Christopher, in my experience, doing leads to being.

I Understand Status Not to Be Something We Are, But Something We Do

There is something to be said about status. The perceived notion that someone is higher up the hierarchy than me. Think about it. Your position in the company and your associated behaviours you show when talking to others. Others' perception of you, and their feelings about their interactions with you. How they respond to you. Said another way, our perceived status affects the degree to which we are willing to be original and hold true to our own principles and values.

Status can also be defined as power dynamics. Status is an ephemeral quality that permeates all aspects of human interaction. Verbal exchanges affect status too, but they are a small part of the equation. Words, actions, clothing, title, and knowledge all combine to define a person's status. I don't believe status is the same as official title or rank. When considering power, I see there being two dimensions or two different sources, positional and personal. These two dimensions do not always go hand in hand. An ineffectual leader may have less actual status than an efficient personal assistant. As a way of looking at relationships, status differences, especially within a business or team, has come to constitute political incorrectness.

Organisations flatten their hierarchies and expect status differentials to disappear. And let's face it, we live in a class society. That's reality. I think it's funny that it's always those with the most power who resist the concept the most strongly. The privileged are often blind to their privileges.

Status exists – all the time, everywhere. I understand status not to be something we are, but something we do. Keith Johnson taught me that in a week-long improvisation masterclass I did a long time ago. In my experience of improv, when actors played high or low status, their work on stage looked more like real-life behaviour. So status is affected by what we do. Humans, like animals, usually have little difficulty reading signs of status and recognising who defers to whom.

In Scouts, I wanted to have all my master grade badges. I liked the fact that there was this floral red leaf around the master grade badge. The standard grade badge was green with a yellow rim around it. But I liked the deep red, and I had to get my master grade everything because of the colour of it. I guess I also wanted the master grade badges because I wanted to be the best at what I was doing. I wanted to make sure that people thought I was good at it – that they perceived me to be higher in status.

I remember doing my master grade cooks, and you had to cook everything on an open fire outside. You had to cook for the entire weekend, and all the scout masters invited other scout masters from other troops. You had to make a certain kind of breakfast, and then you had to make a certain kind of lunch, and then it all culminated in a Sunday roast. Everything had to be cooked on the open fire: roast chicken, roast potatoes, carrots, gravy. And as well as that, you had to have a pudding.

For pudding, I made apple pie, so I built an oven to cook it in. I found a ten-litre paint drum lying around, and I got a hacksaw. I cut through one side of it and bent it open, and then I got another piece of metal which was almost like a tray, and I put it in to make a shelf. And I cooked my apple pie in my makeshift oven, sealing up the oven with the lid and some mud.

For some reason, Brendan, a fellow scout, had a bottle of wine that he was going to serve, and I thought, *oh fuck. I didn't think of that.* So I asked him if I could have some of it to serve with my food, and I thought I'd use this bottle I had. I'd forgotten that what was in the bottle previously was oil. I poured some of his wine into the bottle and poured it for my guests. They didn't drink it. Thankfully, they saw the little bits of oil swimming around at the top. I still got the master grade cooks badge though. They were impressed by my apple pie and my roast chicken and stuff. Brendan didn't get his master cooks badge even with the wine.

Playing the Status Game

Get a bunch of people, maybe a specific team, from the office in a room. Have a pack of playing cards. Give each person in the room a card. Ace is high status and two is low status. Then get them to role-play organising an event of some kind or discussing objectives for the team. However, each person has their card stuck to their foreheads. They are not allowed to see their own card. Everyone must play a role and contribute to the activity at hand. They must relate to each person depending on what card is displayed on a person's forehead. However, they must seek to achieve the task at hand. Notice how people use status to achieve a result. Then finally get them to all stand in a line and arrange themselves in order of high to low status as they perceive their own card to be. The results are interesting.

Debrief with these questions:

1. How did the cards affect the way people spoke to each other?
2. What did you notice about people's responses to one another?
3. Did the task at hand get completed?
4. What might this exercise in your team say about the dynamics at play?
5. What does the exercise say to you about the way individuals operate in a team?
6. What insights do the team have that may be applicable in the office?

I have noticed recently a simple conversation which occurs a lot in business lately. This type of conversation infers a certain status.

"How are you?"

"Busy."

"Yeah, non-stop. There's just not enough time in the day."

"I know. Just so snowed-under at the minute."

I myself have taken part in a conversation like this with a client. I have even told my PA (that I have a PA is hilarious in this context) not to put too many clients in my diary too regularly as it will seem like I am not busy enough. Not high enough in demand.

In a more obvious sense in everyday life, status plays a part. I think about my relationship with my son. I must say, being a dad was always strangely normal. I found it normal from the beginning. Thinking about status, it's quite simple. I've always been his father and not his mate. We have fun, we have a laugh, we cry, we argue, we do things together, and we do things separately, but I'm not his mate. And I never will be. It's the healthiest relationship I have. I think that might be because it's an adult-child relationship, so there's a dependency.

But it's changing. When we become adults, we should have interdependent relationships, but sometimes we get into relationships, even in business, where we are so dependent on other people that we forget who we are. We lose our status.

William and I have a fascinating relationship. We are quite similar. We can go from arguing with each other about something to having the most amount of laughter and fun and happiness. There's also a feeling of joy that I have an influence in someone's life. I have such an impact. Of course, ultimately, he'll make his choices, but those choices are influenced by me and the people around him, and I think that's just wonderful. It's a privilege to be able to have someone like that in your life. I'm here to serve.

Recently, I bought a leather jacket. David thinks I'm trying to channel Kenickie from *Grease*. I get comments like, "*Forty-seven, hmm.*" But I like the leather jacket. In fact, I might even buy a brown one.

William got star of the week at school because of the

consistent effort in his homework, and so with star of the week you get Percy, this little pug toy, and you bring him home. So we went out to dinner, and Percy came with us.

William has this leather jacket that his godparents gave him, and he was wearing his, and I was wearing mine. I said to William, "*Oh look, we're twins.*" Because of the ginger hair and the leather jacket. And his comment to me was simply, "*No, we're not. Because you're forty-seven, and I'm six. And you're tall, and I'm not as tall.*" And I went, "*Oh.*" And he said, "*But we're like twins. Because we both have red hair, and we have both got leather jackets.*"

And it just floored me. I didn't have anything to say. It was the truth. We're not twins, certainly not, but we were *like* twins. In fact, I think he actually said, *looked like twins.* And I thought to myself, *fuck.* A six-year-old was correcting my grammar and making it quite clear what the reality was as opposed to what you think it might be, Daddy. Which is a very good metaphor for my entire life. Isn't status just people's perception of where they fit in the pecking order?

Punishing Hours at the Office

Not so long ago, people would have turned their noses up at a 24/7 dedication to their job or the business. Leisure time was once seen as an indicator of high social status, something attainable only for those at the top. Since the middle of the twentieth century though, things have turned the opposite way – these days, punishing hours at your desk, rather than days off, are seen as the mark of someone important.

When I was reading around the subject of status, I

noticed several experiments where the researchers illustrated just how much we've come to revere busyness, or at least the appearance of it. In the research, volunteers read two vignettes, one about a man who led a life of leisure and another about a man who was overworked and overscheduled. When asked to determine which of the two had a higher social status, the majority of the participants said the latter. The same held true for people who used products that implied they were short on time. In one experiment, for example, customers of the grocery-delivery service were seen as higher status than people who shopped at grocery stores that were equally expensive. In another, people wearing Bluetooth headsets were considered further up on the social ladder than those wearing regular headphones, even when both were just used to listen to music.

However, this may be in part due to the way work itself has changed over the past several decades. The shift from leisure-as-status to busyness-as-status may be linked to the development of knowledge-intensive economies. In such economies, individuals who possess the human capital characteristics that employers or clients value (e.g. competence and ambition) are expected to be in high demand and short supply on the job market. Thus, by telling others that we are busy and working all the time, we are implicitly suggesting that we are sought after, which enhances our perceived status.

I am not suggesting status isn't important. It is. The question is, do you allow your status (or your perception of your status) to be affected by others and/or circumstance? For me growing up, status had a different fallout. Status was about power. Being in control. Or being controlled by others. It was quite absolute. When I was sex-working, I felt I was in control. And I was being controlled during the years of sexual abuse, whilst working manically hard *to* control the situation.

Have you ever felt out of control? Ever felt that others seem to make you do things you know are not right for you? Ever felt like others know more than you? In the context of presenting, speaking, or leading others, ever felt like it's all running away from you? In a job interview and you're sweating like mad? Ever felt like you're out of your depth in a meeting? In the role you are in now - ever felt like an imposter?

In my second last year of primary school, we moved again, and I had to move schools. Again. I spent my last year of primary school at Martin Primary School. It was there I met my friends Brendan and Lesley. Brendan was in the Scouts and St John's Ambulance, so I started to do those things too. And that's how I met Gary. And well you know the story. I felt out of my depth. I was lost. I wasn't able to get out of my situation. My ability to engage with people on an equal level had been destroyed. It was never a level playing field, life isn't, but this playing field was so heavily weighted to a particular team. There was no hope in *playing fair.*

One day, Brendan and I went to Boksburg Lake on our bicycles, and I started talking to this man. I can't remember exactly what he said, but he asked me to go with him and I did. There was this innocent part of me that always saw the good in people. I was still a child. I never saw anyone as dangerous. My first response when I met people was to like them and want to know more about them.

This man took me to this run-down house and took

me into this room. He told me to lie down on this piece of cardboard, so I did. And then he pulled my trousers down, and he raped me. There I was, lying on this cardboard in this derelict house with my pants down. What made me stop it was the smell. Imagine for a moment a grown man penetrating a child from behind. I didn't scream. A deafening silence killed the child that day.

So I stopped it. Oh the pain and disgust! That's what I felt. I jumped up and turned around, and all I could see was his dick covered in shit. I got up and just started running. I never thought of laughing at my fear. But I did then. I ran to my bicycle and pedalled like fuck back to Boksburg Lake. Trapped in a freedom of escape and bewilderment.

When I got back to Brendan, I didn't say anything. I can't remember exactly what was said, but there was a conversation, and we went home. I don't know what Brendan thought. He was there when the chap was talking to me. Brendan didn't talk to him, but I did. I suppose I was that sort of person.

That story is always a tricky one to tell, but using your story takes courage. Bravery. I write this not for sympathy, not to stand on my soapbox and preach, not for self-congratulation – *oh I've made it through. Well done me.* I write this because I promised myself that I would tell the truth, warts and all. I write because perhaps through reading my story, you too can have courage and truly possess the status you deserve. You too can be who you know you are. You too can see you. Sawubona. You too can lead and live with purpose. I write for myself, to be real, like a friend who touches us with a kind and gentle hand.

In business, status matters. Researchers are beginning to quantify just how much. Studies show that companies held in high esteem are able to maintain a significant lead over their rivals. Why does wine from certain parts of the world command higher prices than others? Because of the perceived status (the power of the brand) that particular region has over other wine producing areas.

The same goes for the interview, right? I get dressed up for an interview. Why? Because I want to look nice? Or because I want to look the part? Or because I know that's how they want me to look? At a basic level, it is about status. My perceived view of where I will be in the pecking order. This view has an effect on how they relate to me, and indeed how I respond to them. I know I have gone to interviews in the past when I was working for others knowing I wanted them to see me as having a certain degree of status.

Our social media profiles are another example of status in play. How many likes or shares we get. How many followers etc. A business does well when it's associated with a celebrity. Indeed, associating with a high-status individual or organization is a tried-and-true method of raising one's own stature. We call it public relations. It's just raising your status – placing you on telly.

How Do I Make the Right Status Choices?

We see others getting more likes on Facebook. We see others making more money. People you know being able to buy their second home. We compare ourselves to others to determine our level of success. Comparison is the thief of joy. To what extent do you allow your perception of your status affect what you think and do?

Release the need to compare yourself to others, stand in your own space, and be your own truth.

Are you being original, or are you perpetuating a *me and them* scenario, where you are better than the audience or where your audience is in control? Think about it in terms of your business and your teams. Is the culture of the organisation built on status comparisons?

Human beings are creatures of habit. We become accustomed to doing the small things like standing to the side to let a stranger pass by. And we do these things, like most engagement, without being conscious of what we're doing. If we are feeling a bit down, taking a moment to say hi to another person can interrupt a cycle of negative emotion. If we're greeting someone we've had a conflict with, we can share another more civil side of ourselves and momentarily break the pattern of disagreement. We can momentarily alter how others engage with us. We can momentarily affect how others feel when we have a clear intention about how we will be. We can alter the status game.

We get to know a richer, deeper, more powerful version of who we are when we lose our desire to go through life performing on autopilot. Mindlessly. I know I have. Hanging onto the conventional rituals of engagement can profoundly set us on a path of vanilla. Seth Godin talked about finding your purple cow. What's yours? You? Then be it!

Changing our ritual habits can help us become better people. Better leaders. We must become aware that breaking free from our normal ways of being is what makes it possible to develop different sides of ourselves. Much like I talked about in learning from theatre. We can be present and almost (wanky word warning) trans-formative, allowing us to become a different person for a moment, creating a short-lived alternative reality that returns us to our regular life slightly altered. Not focused on our predetermined view of what we think we must be in comparison to others.

The Practice: Play with Status

Next time you are in a meeting, having a conversation with someone, presenting or speaking at some event, play around with your status. Review the chapter on body language; it will give you some insights into how to physically play with status. But try it with your voice too, referring to the *Circles of Being.*

Remember, start with intent and have the intention to notice what happens when you make conscious status choices. Remind yourself of your purpose and walk into the interaction, the conversation, onto stage etc. with a memorable and motivational intent. Notice:

What happens to your thinking?
What do you do differently?
How do others seem to relate to you?
What feelings come up for you?
Where might you use this approach elsewhere in your life?

Remember to feed-forward:

What did you do well?
What could you do next time to improve?
What are you grateful for?

My Mother Had a Strong Can-Do Attitude

My mother died in 2008. It was fucking horrendous. For a long period of time, she had dementia and Alzheimer's, and it was tricky because she always told me to go and do and work and be away. "*Have fun, Deon. Make your mark.*" She was in Northern Ireland at the time. I have a lot of sadness about it because I don't believe I was there a lot for her towards the end. Someone called Alzheimer's a living death. It is.

She was my rock. People always say that, but she was. She was a real guiding light for me, and I think I learnt my sense of doing from her. Of just being. I will always have a frame in my mind where her memory once was.

The confectionery around the cakes she used to make was amazing. I would watch her make flower petals. She would make individual petals and paint them all, laying them in these egg trays before using egg white to stick them together. They were these perfect, individual-ly-made flowers. The ability to be so present, so intricate with her hands, was amazing. She was an artist. She be-lieved life is about doing things; it's not about sitting back and waiting for things to happen.

My mother had a strong can-do attitude. She had always been about taking action. "*Doing leads to being, Deon,*" she would say. In her line, which she repeated often, "*People are watching, Deon, make your mark, and make it permanent.*" She was saying do *to be* and take responsibility for what you do. You have made the choice. You alone.

I don't think it always came from a place of positive strength though. Sometimes she would say things that seemed in contradiction to her can-do attitude. For example, she also would say, "*The rich get richer, and the poor get poorer.*" She said that line often. And she would say, "*Well, it was all because of your father and that bloody church.*" Or she might say, "*Well, I wasn't very good at school. Joan was always much cleverer than me.*" She had a little chip on her shoulder. It made her real. But she always had an *I will survive* attitude, but more than that thrive.

Mother would get stuck in and do. I think it's because she trusted herself. I think it was because, ultimately, she believed in her capabilities. And I think the same is true of me. I always believe that when I'm doing something I will do it. I believe I can do it. Cooking, tennis, yoga, business, life. It's funny that they're practical things. Not cerebral. My can-do attitude sort of diminishes when it comes to things requiring academic capability. And that's definitely a throwback to school and stuff.

Mother's can-do attitude was almost like a cat falling out of a tree. A cat trusts. It instinctively lands on its feet. It wriggles and does all this kind of breakdancing movement and lands on its feet. I think mother was like that. She would wriggle her way into and out of things. Breakdance her way through life. She would always land on her feet, and I think I have that same inner core self-belief.

She was all about experiencing 'it'. 'It' being life, or even on a smaller scale: that day, that moment, that hour, that conversation. It's funny how my parents could be so different. My mother was always about doing and experiencing, and my father was all about waiting for the hereafter. God bless him, he was filled with depression about the past, of not having achieved what I think he knew he could have, and riddled with anxiety about the future, anxious for redemption.

My father was all about waiting. Let's wait, and our redemption will come. The horridness about that is there's a little part of me that's like him. It fucks me off. But it's mine. It's my choice. Sometimes I'll be waiting for something to happen, and then I realise, fuck no. Let's go and do.

I noticed when growing up that I was always encouraged to get on with things. Although I used to think of my father's constant asking, *"Have you done your homework?"*, *"Have you tidied your room?"*, *"Have you washed the dishes?"* as nagging. I saw him as someone who hadn't achieved much but somehow had a lot to say about other people's shortcomings. He would say, if you don't do this, and if you don't do that, you won't succeed. He was right, from a certain point of view. He just wasn't inspiring me to take action. In fact, it had the opposite effect.

Scouts was about doing. And in my day, we were given a lot of responsibility as young Scouts. I loved Scouts. It was about being outdoors. A sense of freedom. An adventure. A sense of doing something. I think it reminded me of Zimbabwe in some ways. It was outdoorsy and free. And as an adult, I still love camping and being outside.

We went on this one camp in St Lucia, South Africa,

and we went on this three-day hike. I can't remember exactly how, but we lost our food, and we didn't have enough for three days. So we had to go and find some. We hunted guinea fowl and rabbits, and we caught them and skinned them and ate them. It was like the *Famous Five* meets *Bear Grylls*. It's amazing now that I think about it.

Scouts was just an incredible experience because it was all about being outdoors, building rafts, building tents, making stuff, sitting around the campfire and singing songs. That community. That sense of belonging; the spiritual dimension of intelligence. I guess that's why having a sense of openness and freedom and a sense of adventure and fun and excitement is really important to me.

It was all about doing. And I believe through doing we realise who we are because we begin to realise what we like and what we don't like and how we feel about it. As long as we're present.

Casting my mind back to exam time, I remember always – well, perhaps not always but often enough – leaving studying to the last minute, cramming a few days before. And going into a spiral of decline the night before. Actually no, wait, that last bit's a lie. I would be so high on bio-plus that I wouldn't be bothered. There I was in my bedroom, my heart beating like a tom-tom drum, sitting cross-legged at my desk that I had sawn the legs off, making it low to the ground in some ridiculous feng shui experiment. Suffice to say, I procrastinated about anything academic. Even though I had created a study plan some three months earlier. I've always had good intentions. Although, let's face it, good intentions are not the end in themselves.

My father would always say to me, "*Deon, procrastination is the thief of time.*" He was right. It is inaction. It is not doing. It is saying, I will. It is, *when I am eighteen, I will do this. When I have got that first client, I will. When I am...* If I had a £10 for every time I've said, *when I...* I'd be somebody. But I digress. Taking action is the only way. If we are not doing, what are we? Doing is being. Now, I am not only talking about physically taking action; I am talking about thinking action. Getting into the right headspace to do something about it.

Sometimes, if we pay enough attention, our doing is a sign to not do. To find an alternative. To seek a different course. It's exam time, and it's the night before my final biology paper. I have been cramming two years of work into a week. Bear in mind I've been working nights at the Porterhouse (steak house) in Benoni for the past twelve months. So I am not really taking much *study action.* I know what I am meant to do. The thing is, I don't believe. I do not fundamentally believe that I will do well, that I will succeed at this stuff called biology. I am doing this stuff because, "*Deon, boys like you* (what the hell does that mean – boys like me? What, gay boys who haven't come out? Surely not) *must do biology, mathematics, and science. If you don't, you will never amount to anything in this world. And it is a harsh world out there.*" My lack of taking action, in the context of my biology final, resulted in me only just passing.

The action I was taking had nothing to do with biology. It had nothing to do with school. It had everything to do with who I was to be. Everything to do with the person I am today. I was taking action, doing things that I was passionate about, that I loved to do, that I believed in, and therefore, I excelled at doing them. Now don't laugh. The thing I refer to here is waiting tables. That's it simply.

I was cultivating a sense of belief in myself, a sense that I could choose my own path. *My* alternative. I could see *My Game*. Obvs I didn't know it then as I do now. But I could see what I was good at, what I valued.

I could build my own plan and take action. And I was good at it. I was providing the customer with an experience they wanted more of. I had people coming into the Porterhouse asking to be served by me. People drove miles to experience the delicious meal served by me. In fact, after I had eventually left and gone to university (following someone else's plan), I was asked to come back because business had plummeted. Scot, the restaurant owner, said, "*Deon, I need you to come back and help us. The business needs you. People want the Deon experience.*"

Letting go of what you believe you ought to do and stepping into your own identity manifests even on an obvious and simple level, like your job. I found leaving a normal nine-to-five job to be a very positive thing. I gave up what I thought was the 'traditional' way of living and making money and decided to be a jobbing actor. Stepping into my own truth. Although it's tough to relinquish the chains of how you *ought* to live. But it allowed me to do something I really loved to do rather than doing something I had to do. It also gave me a purpose. I think it's a really liberating, wonderfully free mind set to have and experience.

Ever since doing that, I've never really had a nine-to-five job. Since then, I've never really worked for anyone else. When I was a jobbing actor, I was freelancing for other people, but I never saw myself as working for other people. I never saw myself being tied down to something or someone in a work context, and I think that's a wonderful, empowering thing. I was the master of my own destiny, and I could choose to do or not to do.

One of the things I love to help people with now is releasing those perceived shackles of how you must be and who you must be. There is more than one type of prison in this life. I had carried mine around wherever I went. I love helping people to let go of thinking they need a particular kind of job, or that they should behave in a particular kind of way to be successful. There are so many versions of success. Chart your own course. We all compare ourselves to others when we shouldn't. Just because they've been successful doing it that way doesn't mean you have to do it that way too.

I realise this all may sound a little up my own arse. But it is funny what makes certain things people say stick in your mind. Like the things my father said. The things Scot said. And the things we say to ourselves. Hand on heart right here right now, you've been reading the truth about me. I was taking action. The action I wanted. Albeit only for a short while. But my God, it felt good. And I knew it then. What this experience taught me was simply that it is ultimately my responsibility to take action. To do, to be.

To be able to choose, you need to:

1. Realise you can make a choice – acknowledge you have the ability to choose.
2. Make the most useful choice – assess the appropriateness of your available choices.

But the most significant factor in the decision-making process is being *open* to choose. Mindfulness is the only way. Paying attention to what is happening to you. Letting go of the bucket-load of thoughts and feelings we have every second of the day and not hanging onto them gives us space to choose what we place our attention on. So to be able to realise I can make a choice and notice the most useful ones for me, I must:

3. Build a practice of mindful living.

The same goes for speaking. Ain't no point walking into that part of your life on autopilot. Really getting in tune with your breathing before, during, and after speaking can help you make choices driven by your values. Because you are more present, you will notice how you are being and whether this is congruent with your values.

That's why the River of Life exercise is so important.

How Do I Develop My Ability to Choose?

Through observation. By taking notice of yourself. By paying attention. I like the phrase 'taking notice of'. It stands to reason when I take notice, I am taking action. I am being aware and taking responsibility.

As many world-renowned gurus have said, self-awareness and the pursuit thereof takes a lifetime. It is not a complete-able endeavour. It is continual practice of reflection and refinement. Much like public speaking. Much like leadership.

I strongly suggest you use my feed-forward model to help you continually cultivate self-knowing. Use it al the time, in every aspect of your life. In public speaking, presenting, pitching, storytelling, meetings, with family, with colleagues, with suppliers, and especially with yourself. Simply ask yourself these three questions after every interaction with someone. Certainly after an important talk.

What did I do well and should therefore do more of?
What could I do next time to improve?
What am I grateful for?

These uncomplicated three little questions when asked regularly over a lifetime will help you cultivate an ability to make better choices and take deliberate action, living into your true presence.

A Good Story Told Well is Worth More Than Any Amount of *Manure of Data* on a PowerPoint Slide

We all know the rhetoric about a good story. Stories inspire. And we all want to be inspiring. You're a leader. Isn't that the essence of what your role is? When you inspire, you instil trust, or actually, the other way round – when you build trust, you inspire. To fulfil your primary role as a leader – your *in service of others* role in my experience – you have to take your audience for a walk in your shoes.

As I have said countless times in this book, and believe me, a horrendous amount of times in the fifteen plus years I have been doing this work, emotions are everything if you're trying to inspire someone. What does Luke Skywalker say? "*Breathe. Reach out with your feelings.*" If you're trying to build trust, if you want to *reach out*, the best way is by using personal stories.

One recent poignant story was when I was back in South Africa with my family. I rekindled relationships with family that I haven't had in years. Over ten years. Some even in twenty years. It reinforced for me that we as human beings are inherently kind. We just get caught up with so many other things in life. We lose sight of the things that matter, and at the heart of it is kindness to one another.

And it was emotional, even setting aside the obvious emotional rollercoaster, to see my cousin Julian. Last time I saw him, albeit I don't remember, was at my other cousin's wedding in 1977. So I was six, Julian was five, and my brother was eight. And it's strange that Julian and I can be related but not have anything in common and be strangers to one another.

It felt overwhelming at times. One Saturday afternoon, the whole lot (and I mean at least twenty of them) came over for a barbecue (aka braai) at my cousin's place in Johannesburg. Very lovely house with pool and tennis court. There we were standing around having a barbecue, and the men were standing around drinking beers and having men chat. And I sort of sauntered over, made it very camp, and made a joke, trying to break the ice. Much like I did with the *football dads*. Silence. Deathly silence. Clearly in this moment I hadn't made a good enough connection. We really didn't know each other. The conversation continued, and the banter started flowing. I dropped in another playful gay and decidedly camp story, and boom! I smashed it. Know your audience. It was the right story delivered at the right time.

Now I am not suggesting playing for the laugh. Earlier, I suggested when I was an improv actor that playing for the laugh would destroy the scene, end the story. But in this case, the context and the intention was different. Having a laugh was why we were standing around the braai.

There are some key elements to good story-sharing as I like to call it. I call it this because telling appears one-sided. The key elements are:

- Have a clear intent, a reason for speaking. It should

stem from your purpose.

- Know your audience and understand your call to action.
- You shouldn't include everything; in fact, less is more.
- Always use your personal stories/anecdotes to convey core messages. When you do this, you own the talk. You own what you are saying.
- Bring true emotion to bear. People relate to emotion. We connect to it. We are driven by it. Any talk devoid of emotion isn't worth listening to. And certainly isn't worth delivering.

I am sure you have been to an event where the speaker drones on and on. And they seem competent. They are making good eye contact. Their voice is projecting well. They are using the space well, not pacing up and down. Their content is brilliant. But you switch off. You're not engaged. You're not investing in it. They aren't invested in themselves.

While I was in South Africa, I spent some time with Allan, my brother, which was really good. That's the longest Allan and I have spent together – seven days – in the last twenty-odd years. So we sat together one afternoon in a restaurant, and for the first time, Allan and I actually had a conversation about the sexual abuse I experienced. It was good to have the conversation, but it was a very emotional thing because he got quite upset about it. I think he knew of it, but he didn't know any of the details. It's had a real positive effect on us, on our relationship.

Stories have the power to connect, to change people, to

change lives. Stories change the way we see ourselves, the way we see each other. Stories change the world.

There is a Science to Story-Sharing

It is quiet and dark. The cinema is hushed. I'm watching James Bond, a Daniel Craig one – droolingly delicious! He skirts along the edge of a building as his enemy takes aim. Here in the audience, heart rates increase, and palms sweat. I can feel the energy; it's palpable. I am watching people's reactions to the antics on screen. It's okay, I've seen the film nearly a dozen times. I'm doing my research. Clearly not very scientific. I am measuring the brain activity of a dozen viewers. I am watching an amazing neural ballet in which a storyline changes the activity of people's brains.

We all get the power of story-sharing in a practical sense – we have observed how compelling a well-constructed narrative can be. But recent science has begun to put a much finer point on just how stories change our attitudes, beliefs, and behaviours.

As social creatures, we depend on others for our survival and happiness. A decade or so ago, scientists discovered a neurochemical called oxytocin which is a key 'it's safe to approach others' signal in the brain. Now, I am no scientist, but I do know that oxytocin is produced when we are trusted or shown a kindness, and it motivates cooperation with others. It does this by enhancing the sense of empathy, our ability to experience others' emotions. Empathy is important for us social creatures because it allows us to understand how others are likely to react to a situation, including those with whom we work.

More recently, they (the scientists) have concluded you can 'hack' the oxytocin system to motivate people to engage in cooperative behaviours. They found that character-driven stories consistently caused oxytocin synthesis. And the more oxytocin released by the brain had an impact on how much people were willing to help others: for example, donating money to a charity associated with the narrative.

Further evidence proves that in order to motivate a desire to help others, a story must first sustain attention – a scarce resource in the brain – by developing tension during the narrative. If the story is able to create that tension, then it's likely that attentive viewers/listeners will come to share the emotions of the characters in it, and after it ends, likely to continue mimicking the feelings and behaviours of those characters. This explains the feeling of dominance I have after watching James Bond save the world, as well as the fact that Daniel is so delish.

So as a leader, you need to be using character-driven stories with emotional content to bring about a better understanding of what you want your audience to do, be it in a one-to-one or team meeting or in a formal presenting sense. If you do this, the audience will be better able to recall the main points weeks later. In terms of making impact, this fucks with the standard PowerPoint presentation, right? So as I have said to so many of my clients, begin every presentation with a compelling, human-scale story. In other words, why should customers or a person on the street care about the project you are proposing? How does it change the world or improve lives? How will people feel when it is complete? These are the components that make information persuasive and memorable.

In my humble opinion, your story, the narrative of it when told authentically, will help the people you lead navigate the world in which they operate – to know where they are coming from and where they are headed. It tells them where to place their trust and why. Think about it for a minute. The reason we love fiction is that it enables us to find our bearings in possible future realities or to make better sense of our own past experiences. What stories give us, in the end, is reassurance. And as childish as it may seem, that sense of security – that coherent sense of self – is essential to our survival. Why wouldn't you want that for yourself, for the people you mean to inspire and lead?

Some of the most impactful talks I've heard have focused on overcoming adversity. But this is one topic that lots of leaders seem to shy away from. Maybe it has something to do with some sense of shame, or a sense of failure, or just not wanting to air the dirty laundry, not wanting to look vulnerable. But here's the thing, everyone (yes, everyone) has a past, and that past will have had some amount of adversity. It doesn't have to be as heavy as mine.

I realised I don't have to show the world I am good. I don't have to try to hide the things I've done that are not quite flattering – and there have been plenty. I just need to forgive and accept myself and trust. That's the truth of leadership. I don't know about you, but I have spent far too many years of my life pretending and trying to maintain an illusion I am something other than me. The virus of self-censorship. I'd rather be real with people and know the ones who accept me, who get me, accept me fully, than pretend. Warts and all. When you are telling your stories, own them. Feel them, be them. Feel the force, baby.

To connect, to establish rapport, and ultimately inspire, you need to establish a common bond with the audience. That's why tales of adversity and overcoming adversity can pay off. And everyone's story, even if it has a common theme, will be different. But if you're trying to get across a new idea, or challenging the audience to think differently, then they will only grasp a new or alien concept through the story of one individual. And that individual obvs would be you.

Essentially, your story will help your audience walk a mile in your own shoes. And that mile-long journey is the distance you need to take your audience to get them on your wavelength. Story-sharing in leadership isn't just to 'entertain'. Stories can be used to get teams to see things from a different perspective, and that's the start of the process to change how they feel.

Things don't always go to plan in life or in business. But you can reframe the experience and *own* your story and share it with real purpose. Inspirational leaders spend a lot of time reflecting on their own lives. And when I say inspirational speakers, I'm not talking about 'super humans'. They're not all Olympians or astronauts. They're people like you.

Let me tell you about Vicky. Recently, I came back from a week away studying NLP. Yip, I too have done it. What? It's good to explore one's own skills too. Add more strings to your bow.

There was Vicky. Was she an industry leader? An entrepreneur? No. She was a young women who worked for a local charity. She wasn't all razzmatazz and show. She wasn't a millionaire. She was Vicky. And boy, did Vicky have a story.

She spoke simply, almost matter-of-factly. There was no artifice. No staging. No 'show'. You could hear a pin drop as she spoke. In the space of twenty-five minutes while Vicky spoke, I felt my perspective start to change on the issues of addiction, loss, abuse, and the power of individual choice. Vicky was the most inspiring speaker I had ever heard. And Vicky didn't even know she had that power. The humility blew me away. Vicky was a true model of taking action, driving-principle, and being a leader. Today, Vicky works with clients struggling with addiction and homelessness. She has turned her story of adversity into something with real meaning and power. And she is making a difference.

So what about you? Your story. Your truth. Using your River of Life and your reservoir of stories, you too can make a difference. You can be the one people remember. You can be the one building trusting relationships. I believe lots of people have that power, you included. Your own personal journey and your own values can do the talking for you, and it's about honing the craft of speaking your truth to help you stand out from the crowd.

Let's look at story-sharing in a lot more detail. Try out these exercises. Remember, practice them. Build your stories using a framework that suits you. Begin to reflect on the stories you have told. You can also use this framework to ensure your anecdotes have the core elements of a good story. These simple frameworks will make for rich and rewarding story-sharing.

Stories are compelling. They are unique. Facts and knowledge can be disputed. Your stories are yours. They cannot be disputed.

Stories engage, connect, challenge, and move an audience to think, feel, or do something. When truth-telling, it is important to remember that the audience will interpret your stories in their own way.

There are a number of ways to explore the core elements of good story-sharing. But you must always start with 'why'. Remember, intent is simply asking yourself, *why* am I speaking? It is your motivation for standing up and talking.

Firstly, the…

Purpose – why *this* particular story? Make sure your story fits with your overall intent and call to action.

Then the…

Place – what action happened and where does it take place? Describe, with as much detail as you can, the action of events. The moment to moment happenings. Add into this the locations, even going as far as naming them. This anchors the story in a reality that is translatable.

Then finally…

People – who was there, and what did they think and feel? This is all about the characters in your story. Their emotional experience. This needs to be delivered with language that is appropriately emotive. Appropriate to your intent or purpose. Remember the scale: one being dull emotionless and ten being totes inappropriate.

This is where the audience connects with what you are saying in a manner that is personal for them. This element makes the difference between presenting by numbers or going through some automatic notion of presenting versus having a conversation an audience and connecting with them.

Another way to describe the three Ps of story-sharing is to look at this craft using characterisation of the *villain* the *victim*, and the *hero.* Every good story from time and memorial has these three elements in it.

Again, think *Star Wars* for a moment. It is *not* a story about intergalactic battles and Stormtroopers. It is a story about a hero, Luke Skywalker, overcoming the villain Darth Vader, to return the victim, Princess Leia, to her home world. We are drawn in by Luke's purpose, his intent on saving her from Darth Vader. We are taken on a journey to interstellar locations with wonderfully strange and delightful characters, people. We get to know these people. What they think and how they feel. We connect with these people. They have similar emotional responses and thoughts as we do. We buy into the story.

You in your presentation or public speaking talk are the hero. Be sure to present yourself as such without ego but driven by your personal values. Let the thing that frustrates your audience (your clients) be the villain. And your clients or your audience are the victims.

My client Samantha is a botanist. She speaks regularly, mainly on panels at science fairs around the globe. knew there was something about her people are drawn to Call it charisma or an energy. A force. A presence.

We spent a great deal of time together over six months Having a one-to-one session with Samantha recently, was struck by her ability to notice her conscious thoughts and feelings when speaking.

"I really notice I start everything with my story. I notice the story structure. I know instantly what story to tell. I am so much more aware of the relevance certain stories can have for the audience and my message. I use them to drive home my messages."

She was talking about a particular recent panel she was on. We discussed how she felt about 'being assertive' with her story and seemingly disagreeing with other members of the panel.

"With a story framework, I am more confident in making my point in the story. I am just much more aware of my message, the stories I can use to get my message across, and how to do it in a relevant way. It's been trial and error though."

Samantha's conscious awareness helped her keep a check on reality. She knew she could be opinionated and articulate a point with a certain assertiveness. We talked through why she felt at times as though she was 'too pushy'. We explored how she could notice these thoughts and feelings and let them go if they didn't serve her.

Adding Colour and Advance When Speaking

I am fascinated by the way people tell stories. We have been telling them since the world began. Since the beginnings of the spoken word and before. Have you ever sat in a public place – a pub, restaurant, or even just in the shopping mall waiting for your other half – and watched people? Watched how they interact. Listened to their stories. Sounds a bit creepy, but it amazes me.

If you do end up doing this creepy eavesdropping exercise, you will notice people don't just provide factual information. They share wonderfully intricate nuances and names of people. The story is filled with colour. They describe the place in real detail, including specific timings and textures. Oh, it is totally driven by why they are telling the story. Their desire. Their intention. Colouring a story adds emotion and depth. We connect to this depth. It is a very right brain experience.

The Practice: Colour and Advance

Next time you are out at a pub, restaurant, or just talking to friends, start to notice the way you embellish the stories you share. Begin to make conscious choices about the use of emotion and factual information in your storytelling. For example:

Kathy left to go home. When she got home, she unpacked her shopping, put the kettle on, and put the shopping away. She sat down and had a cup of tea with a slice of cake.

And how often you may embellish the story further:

Kathy got home exhausted and feeling really angry. She began to unpack her shopping with gusto. She didn't want to spend the next hour doing it. She had other plans. Plans for a delicious slice of cake, which she had just bought. And a hot cup of tea. She put the kettle on. It was her favourite thing to do, relax with a slice of Madeira cake and a cuppa. Put her feet up and let go all the frustrations of shopping just before Christmas.

Have the intention to understand the techniques of adding emotion and feeling and marrying facts and information to create a powerful story. Pay attention to your use of emotional language and facts when you are telling stories. Neither are wrong. Both have equal value in storytelling.

Colour adds emotion and feeling. It adds depth and meaning to your story. Advance provides facts and information. It moves your truth along.

Both are equally important. There isn't a hard and fast rule to when you should colour or when you should advance. Although a rule of thumb is that you should mix it up. Sometimes you might advance for a while. Sometimes you might colour for a bit. Other moments you may do both at the same time just like the example above.

Reflection Questions/Points:

1. When colouring and advancing in your storytelling, what have you noticed happens to your audience's responses?
2. Notice when you colour and advance when telling everyday stories at dinner or down the pub.
3. Make a point to colour if you generally present factual information or if you notice you move presentations along quickly.
4. Where might you use some of this new-found awareness of colouring and advancing when speaking?

Remember to feed-forward:

Ask yourself...

1. What did I do well that I should do more of?
2. What could I do to improve next time?
3. What am I grateful for in myself?

We Are the Essence of the Person We Were at Our Seventh Birthday Party as on Our Wedding Day and at Our Retirement Celebration

My past actions have most certainly shaped today, but I am not what I've been, positive or negative. I know now I don't need to carry around labels or mistakes from yesterday as if they define me. Whatever I've done, it's over. It doesn't have to brand me, particularly not if I'm making the conscious choice to do things differently now.

My dad dying in 2017, and returning to South Africa for the funeral, reinforced my belief in the power of relationships. The true value of human kindness.

Looking back on my recent trip to South Africa got me thinking. I was getting a little nostalgic. Being nostalgic isn't just a soppy emotion – it has amplified the best and worst in me. Nostalgia has its value for leadership in that time can be a healer. Think about nostalgia generally. Endless movie remakes. I do not know how many times I have watched *Out of Africa*. The return of baby names last in fashion a century ago. Politicians who seem to want to turn the clock back to *that* era. It seems, the past has never been more popular than at present. Even Brexit is argued as harping back to a past time. Not making a political statement here!

At times, harmless nostalgia can also be a powerful motivator of all that is good and bad in humanity. It is not a static feeling, pinned to the past, but a galvanising force, shaping the future and your future business success. Nostalgia can provoke political upheaval, xenophobia, and bitter tribalism, yet, as psychologists are coming to understand, it can also promote well-being, tolerance and a sense of meaningfulness in life. Used in the right way, it can drive teams to achieve more. It certainly has driven me to success.

I was talking to a client the other day about what it takes to truly galvanise a team. He had a team (a business) of over two hundred. People from all walks of life. Adrian posed this question: *How do I know if I am right for this business?* By the way, he turned the business round from a year-on-year loss to generating annual cash profits of some £50 million. But hey, money isn't everything.

I thought, at this moment he wants my view, not some coaching question where I throw his question back at him. I said, "*I can judge myself and others by either my weakest moments or my strongest. It is my choice. When I choose to focus on the strongest and leverage that pride for more of those moments, I am connected. I see me. The essence of me. Every time I feel good about what I do, it's one more reminder to love who I am.*"

I went on to say, "*Growing up in the white suburbs of apartheid South Africa, a country and community committed to not seeing, showed me how toxic denial can be. It's denial that makes fifty years of racist legislation possible while people convince themselves that they are doing nothing wrong. I learned, first hand, of the destructive power of denial at a personal level* before I understood what it was doing to *South Africa*."

We continued our discussion. I talked to him about my longing for my lost teenage years from being sexually abused, and my joy at the birth of my son. Nostalgia is not some rare affliction but an emotion found in all cultures. At once a mixture of happiness and longing, its bittersweet nature is unique but universal, and therefore has the power to bring people together.

Reflecting on nostalgic events you have experienced forges bonds with other people and enhances positive feelings and self-esteem. Being in South Africa brought back wonderful memories of childhood. Memories of sitting on my dad's knee with Allan on the other and Dad reading the *Tank Engine* books. Playing football outside. Dad and I against Allan and his best friend, Darren. Dad and I were Ipswich, and they were Liverpool. It was the 1980s. Happiness.

But sadness too as Dad and I hadn't spoken since my mother died some ten years ago. We had no relationship. He had no relationship with my son. He had with his other grandchildren. And there Allan and I were amongst people my dad knew (we didn't), and they loved him. We were together in our grief and celebration of my father's life.

I believe nostalgia gives us a sense of continuity in life. While so much in our lives can change – jobs, where we live, relationships – nostalgia reminds us that we are the essence of the person we were at our seventh birthday party as on our wedding day and at our retirement celebration.

I was recently at one of my favourite client's business

anniversary event. It was a lavish affair, fabulous, held in the Natural History Museum. If you haven't seen inside this building in London, you should, it is stunningly beautiful. There I was with about five hundred guests reminiscing about the business' successes over the past forty years. As well as some of the not so good bits. There was plenty of wine and delicious food too. We were being nostalgic. We crave it; it is a very human thing. Think about it, what is a story if it is not a series of nostalgic events.

When we tell stories, we are being nostalgic. We are ruminating about past events, usually positively. And when people feel uncertain or uncomfortable or unsure, they might use their memories as a stabilising force. They will create nostalgic memories, which are emotion-full. Think about your summer holidays, family trips, or that successful pitch for new business. We harp back.

I believe while some of us are more prone to nostalgia than others, most of us experience it at least once a week. I see nostalgia is an antidote to loneliness, not its cause. It springs up when we are feeling low, and in general boosts well-being. I have found that reflecting on nostalgic events I have experienced (this book for one) forges bonds with other people and enhances positive feelings and self-esteem.

What's the Value then for Teams and Business?

Nostalgia is a resource and can be a force for future success. Whether or not you are very nostalgic, you can reap the emotion's benefits by triggering it in yourself and your business.

My research (I use this term in its broadest sense – my work isn't empirical research) has shown that a leader's truth is useful inside an organisation. We know that people are substantially more motivated by their organisation's transcendent purpose, in other words, how it improves lives, rather than by its transactional undertakings (how it sells goods and services).

Let's think about Steve Jobs. He didn't care too much about talking about what Apple did. What he cared most about was why Apple did what it did. My interpretation of Steve Job's transcendent purpose was that he wanted to fuck with the status quo. Transcendent purpose is effectively communicated through stories – for example, by describing the pitiable situations of actual, named customers and how their problems were solved by your efforts.

Using your own emotion and feelings appropriately will ensure your people empathise with the pain the customer experienced, and they will also feel the pleasure of its resolution – even more if some heroics went in to reducing suffering or struggle or producing joy. We know that enduring stories tend to share a dramatic arc in which a character struggles and eventually finds heretofore (love this word, makes me feel clever) unknown abilities and uses these to triumph over adversity; the brain is highly attracted to this story style.

And don't forget that your organisation has its own story – its founding myth. It is one of its most power leadership tools. An effective way to communicate transcendent purpose is by sharing that tale. What passion led the founder(s) to risk health and wealth to start the enterprise? Why was it so important, and what barriers had to be overcome? This is your purpose. These are the stories that, repeated over and over, stay core to the organisation's DNA. They provide guidance for daily decision-making as well as the motivation that comes with the conviction that the organisation's work must go on and needs everyone's full engagement to make a difference in people's lives.

When you want to motivate, persuade, or be remembered, start with a story of human struggle and eventual triumph. It will capture people's hearts by first attracting their brains. Doing the River of Life exercise will help you discover the gems of stories in your experiences. It gives you a gateway to the past, which has meaning for the present and can help set a trajectory for the future.

There's No Need to Live in the Past

The past (your River of Life, and dare I say your exec team's too) can provide valuable insights for the present and the future. I just tweeted that today in response to an article written by Sir Richard Branson. He talked about looking to the horizon all the time whilst learning from the past. I agree with using the past with a focus on the present to drive you towards the future.

As Branson suggested, keep your eyes on the horizon. I hear some version of this sentiment all the time from the executives I work with. When the history of an organisation does come up, it's usually about an anniversary – just part of the *balloons and fireworks* as one business leader I know characterised his company's bicentennial celebration. This is not to say that celebrations are unimportant. A fast-changing world appears to leave little time for nostalgia and irrelevant details, but nostalgia has it value.

Leaders with no patience for history are missing a vital truth. A sophisticated understanding of the past is one of the most powerful tools you have for shaping the future. Consider how Kraft Foods managed its 2010 integration of the British confectioner Cadbury. Cadbury's management had mounted fierce resistance to the acquisition, and many of its 45,000 employees feared the loss of their values and an end to the product quality for which the company was known. As the clash of cultures was picked up by the business press, many observers predicted that this would prove to be yet another value-destroying deal, a nightmare of post-merger failure to integrate.

They deliberately used the company's history to ease anxiety, but the story only begins to explain how a company can utilise its past. The job of leaders, most would agree, is to inspire collective efforts and devise smart strategies for the future. History can be profitably employed on both fronts. As a leader strives to get people working together productively, communicating the history of the enterprise can instil a sense of identity and purpose and suggest the goals that will resonate. In its most familiar form, as a narrative about the past, history is a rich explanatory tool with which executives can make a case for change and motivate people to overcome challenges.

Alan, a CEO of a software firm based in the UK that I work with, has taken this to a higher level. Alan uses it as a potent problem-solving tool, one that offers pragmatic insights, valid generalizations, and meaningful perspectives – a way through management fads and the noise of the moment to what really matters. For him the challenge was to find in his organisation's history its *usable* past. This I believe starts with *his* purpose. And *his* personal story.

Recalling Your History to Unite and Inspire People

Alan's decision to invoke the past to pull people together may have been intuitive, but his company's success was consistent with a finding of many scholars. A shared history is a large part of what binds individuals into a community and imbues a group with a distinct identity. I have one being white South African. I don't like it but it is mine. Alan and I worked on some content he could use to engage employees. We created enough content for what we called his roadshow. He went out there and talked about the organisation's history, which helped employees understand what was happening around them. "*The present,*" according to the historian and philosopher David Carr, "*gets its sense from the background of comparable events to which it belongs.*"

At my cousin's house, at that braai, we reminisced about times past. Laughing and joking and feeling sad about my father's death.

Knowing the history of a group to which we belong can help us see events, and ourselves, as part of a still unfolding story and of something larger than ourselves. Likewise, the same applies to individuals. When we understand what is important to us about our past narrative, we can use this to shape our present and future.

It's obvious, right? One use of organisational history then is simply to remind people who we are. The bond is so strong in groups that historical anecdotes making the rounds can come to constitute a truthful mythology, with or without the sanction of a group's leaders. Companies young and old have their creation myths and cautionary tales – typically stories about entrepreneurs and risk takers, about triumph over adversity, about perseverance and sometimes just survival.

Why Do Stories Get Repeated?

Why do stories about the organisation's past get repeated? Why do we repeatedly tell stories about our past? Because it says something positive about the values that people want to preserve. It says something about who we are and what we stand for. In my humble opinion, once leaders recognise how history shapes culture, the importance of learning lessons from the past becomes clear. Using the River of Life exercise helps to understand where we have come from.

One of my clients once said to me, *"We believe it is essential for every one of our partners and colleagues to understand our history and how our values were shaped over time. Although the context today is radically different from what it was twenty years ago, we can still draw lessons from understanding how previous generations of partners confronted challenges and opportunities and responded to them. The past is a kind of screen upon which we project our vision of the future."*

Even when no clear picture of the future can be discerned in the past, leaders can use their stories to explain how the organisation has arrived at a critical need for change through no fault of current management or employees and why the sometimes painful steps that follow are necessary in a larger process of change and adaptation. Your River of Life, your executive team's, and your company's story can be used to put adversity in context and to help heal rifts.

Thinking Like a Historian

The reality is that we are all historians when it comes to making decisions. The ability to identify opportunities or problems in the present (and to frame aspirations for the future) inevitably grows out of personal experience augmented by our broader societal knowledge of what has come before. How can you know where you're going if you don't know where you've been?

So it doesn't surprise me when I work with business leaders that many, regardless of their educational background, think like historians. They start with an insistence on basing any serious decision on facts. To be a good historian demands treating facts with intellectual integrity – viewing them with an open mind and a willingness to be surprised. History also impels us to think about the long term – another strength of the best leaders, whose well-developed, long-range perspective on the companies they manage may be the only antidote to the pressures of quarterly earnings reporting and the need to react to one crisis (real or perceived) after another.

An old saying, frequently attributed to Mark Twain, is, *History does not repeat itself, but it often rhymes.* That is why we also search for useful analogues in history. For it is in the rhyming, the patterns, we can find perspective on the dimensions of our challenges and on the questions we must pose in order to progress. You too have a rhythm in your truth. Use it to create a story that chimes with your employees, clients, and stakeholders alike.

Here are my three action points to creating a culture where stories connect:

1. Create a consciousness in the business, a willingness to look back at events and allow individuals to voice their nostalgic emotions. Allow them to reminisce about their feelings, good and bad.
2. Use these feelings and emotions to build trust with one another, building a sense of freedom, happiness, and cohesion.
3. As a leader, be vulnerable. Get out there with your teams and show your emotions. Talk to your people about your emotions and feelings of sadness and happiness about the business' past experiences. Use this to boost well-being in the team and galvanise tolerance for change and a sense of meaningfulness in life and in the future of business.

How We See Ourselves is the Main Determining Factor of the Way Others Perceive Us

When I got a job as the deputy store manager at an international retail outlet in Belfast, Jeanette and I started going out clubbing. I had my first E then. It must have been 1996. I fucking loved them. I thought they were amazing. I am not advocating taking drugs. Drugs are bad. End of.

I got to the point where I wanted to go out every single weekend, and all I wanted to do was take drugs. I was addicted. I got help for the addiction, but that was much later. My habit was racing through the week to get to the weekend high. The weekend high soon became a daily high. A delicious life-churning cocktail of drugs and anti-depressants. Of course, it made me feel great, but there was another side to it: I wanted to have sex with my wife. Masking my true feelings. The truth I knew I had to face but hadn't. And it became so consuming that I started to steal money.

As the deputy store manager, I had to sign any refunds that were made. It was either Cathy, the store manager, or me who had to sign them. So I started to make false refunds. It was a lot of money. That's how I fuelled my addiction. It would have been more, but I got caught.

They brought this chap over from England. I came into

the store, and as usual, I went to the till to check on the rota. Cathy came from the back, and I said good morning and she just ignored me. I had had my daily cocktail of coke and Prozac. No-one knew my secrets. *What's wrong with me? Nothing. Why do I do this? Ah, never mind.* I was perfectly high. She walked straight out of the store. Then the chap came from the back and said, "*Do you want to come to the back and have a chat, Deon?*" Fuck. I knew it. The walls came down. Like a metal shop-shutter. The monster was going to break out. And it was coming after me.

They confronted me. There were all these receipts with my signature on, but I denied it. I denied it. I denied it. Until eventually they got me to confess and write a statement.

They escorted me off the property, and I went crying to Jeanette that I'd been fired. I told her it wasn't me, and repeated that lie in court. I didn't think about that at the time. My marshmallowed-brain fried to within inches of insanity. It wasn't calculated; it was a fight or flight situation. That just happened to become the story. I was an addict. Addicted to drugs, to lying, deceit, to not living my truth. I didn't know how the fuck I was going to get out of it. I was guilty. I was wrong. I stole money.

Then a few days later. High, I got a phone call from a detective asking me to come into Musgrave Police Station. *Shit how do I do this?* Before arriving for my police interview I took my usual cocktail, like some sort of aperitif. I was arrested, and I denied the whole thing. I said it was someone else. I blamed a woman who worked in the store with me. I said sometimes she would come up to me and get me to sign something that she had refunded because it had to have my signature. This did happen, a number of staff would do this, but I used their honest actions to create a smokescreen of deceit.

Eventually, they charged me with theft, but my story was that this woman did it. I went to court, and she had to come and testify when I was accusing her of doing something she didn't do. Finally, I gave up on the lie, and I came clean. Because I'd lied and stolen and disrupted the course of justice, I was going to go to prison. My lawyer pleaded on the grounds of temporary insanity due to drug addiction. Not insane but going through a lot of trauma. In the end, I got a conditional sentence for three years. And was made to get help with the addiction. I did. It was my first offense. My only.

I had already seen the bottom. In this, one of my darkest hours I still knew deep down I had nothing to fear. But lies destroy. Untruths mask the fraudulence. I did wrong. I betrayed the trust in myself and destroyed any trust others might have had in me. The pain of dishonesty still haunts me today, like a festering sore. A scab of shame. Never again will I wear a mask of deceit. Never again will I merely exist. I want to live as me. When I have lived my truth, things have fallen into place. When I have stopped listening to Mr Doubt and responded to Mrs Belief, I'm in the zone. In flow. It – life – is effortless. When I play to my strengths and live my values and rely on my intuition and tap into my people (my tribe), I am in flow. I'm living intentionally. Think *My Game*: (S+V) I = P.

Leading intentionally, not to sound too deep and meaningful, but I am going to...the stars align. I feel aligned and connected to the right things. Not an ego-driven existence. Nothing was aligned for me for so long. With *alignment with self,* you can build real trust in relationships and organisations. Sometimes building truthful, trusting relationships is often mischaracterised as a soft skill primarily focused on creating warmth and fuzziness. The reality is, trust has hard, bottom-line benefits for organisations.

There are plenty of leadership books out there that tell a better story about the impact of mistrust. And we have certainly heard a great deal about the global impact of mistrust across an industry, resulting in the 2008 crash. Ultimately, you want to be remembered, right? For what? You want even more success? You may even want to improve business performance. You may want to improve humankind. Rid the world of poverty. Make loads of money. Change the way people relate to one another. Ultimately, what we all want is to feel trusted and to trust.

It is about being original. Be the true you. Know why you are here, your purpose. Who you are in the movie of your life, but also in every scene; who you are moment to moment when talking to others. Know how you want to show up and be. Nothing to do with how others perceive you. You can't do much about their perception.

When we know who we truly are, we can be present in the world. We can live an intent-driven life, ridding ourselves of the expectations we place on ourselves and beginning to measure our self-worth by our own internal compass.

We Don't Need to Benchmark
Ourselves or Our Business

Over the years, I noticed I confused an inner steely determination and strength with self-value. They are not the same. Much like me swimming the hundred fly. This self-comparison we all do, right? In business, we call it benchmarking. And it is a vitally important consideration for business success. Right? Where are we compared to our competitors?

I say bollocks to that! Why do you need to research what others are doing? To validate what we are doing ourselves? To check that I can do as good a job? Why? To differentiate ourselves? Because we are needy? We want affirmation. We want acknowledgement. We want praise and reward.

Whatever happened to true self-belief? Believing in yourself and in your plan. Saying not, I cannot, but I can...and the rest. When we are being original, our true self in every dimension of our lives, when we are being authentic – to thine own self be true – we are relevant. We are powerful. We then loose the desire to overcompensate. Less becomes more.

Think about a famous brand you recognise that stands out from the crowd. A famous product. I can think of plenty. What is it that makes them stand out? I suggest they seem original. The dictionary defines original as present or existing from the beginning: first or earliest. The noun is the earliest form of something, from which copies may be made. Synonyms include authentic, bona fide, actual, real, true, genuine etc. So you have a product in mind. What makes that product brand so recognisable? What are its qualities? In a sentence, it lives up to its brand image. Well, the very successful ones do. They simply are what they are.

Think about this in the context of you as person. As a leader. Are you what you truly are? Are you *the* original? Or do you purport one message and live another? I know what it feels like to do this. I lived for twenty-eight years of my life portraying a certain message. I needed drugs to help me be what I believed I ought to be. I needed to steal to fuel a perceived authenticity. I lived someone else's life. What I believed to be what others expected of me. I did not believe in myself and in my plan. I crawled my way through the African jungle on my belly never looking up over the grassy savannah to see the beauty of the African wildlife. I couldn't say sawubona to myself, let alone to anyone else. My point here comes back to the learning from theatre analogy. You may think you are being your true self, however, if that which you are doing, thinking, and feeling is derived from what you believe others expect of you, you're not. I know you know this, but do you live it? How we see ourselves is the main determining factor of the way others perceive us. I see me, and I *see* you. What do you see?

I Was Evangelical Because It Was Important to Me

The implications of living through others' expectations are immense. Or indeed your own perception of what you think others' expectations of you are. I think some-times that last sentence can be a bit of a head-fuck. It's perception. Certainly in business others' expectations can be huge.

I remember my first big job in the City. I was appointed HR Director for a very large commercial enterprise with a turnover of around £250 million. Shit the bed! I know, mega.

The day before I was about to present the L&D strategy to the board, I chickened out. Well, I chickened out to a point. I presented to the board. I failed. It was awful. On reflection, I think it was one of my really low points in business. In fact, dare I say, worse than my business failures. It was that bad because I wasn't me, and I knew it. I was being someone I believed they wanted me to be. resigned the very next day.

Emma and I used to do this play to help bring some of the principles of our truthful leadership model to life. It was called *The Gathering*. We would adapt it to make it relevant and appropriate to the company, and we would use it as an introduction to the session for the day, and we would use it to unpick the principles. It was a gathering of senior people coming together, and there were five actors, and it would only last for half an hour.

One of the pieces of feedback we got from this particular client at the end of the day was that I was too evangelical. We never worked with them again. Emma still jokes with me about it and takes the piss in as much as, *you haven't let that go, have you, Deon?* Talk about mindfulness. Letting go. And I hadn't in a way. It took me a long time to let it go because of that strong desire for belonging, for validation. But I was evangelical because the messages in that play, in this book, are important to me. It's important for people to be their truth, to live as their true self, to find it.

So how do I live the true me? I personally hate the

seven steps to success, the five answers to enlightenment etc. But here are my five pence worth for being the real me:

1. Know the why of what you are about to do in each moment. Get a handle on your intent and purpose (your maxim for life).
2. Understand your values. Know what is important to you. Know where your values come from – mine your life experiences for real clarification.
3. Live your values. Use the stories that surround your values to convey who you are. Be true to these stories. Don't just speak about them. Live them.
4. Meditate and reflect on the impact the above has on you and the people around you. Make the necessary changes as and when.
5. Show emotion. Allow yourself to feel. Learn how others feel and use this to understand yourself and others better.

Live the My Game formula: (S+V) I = P. The truth of leadership is to know yourself, trust yourself, and be yourself; only then will you be truly trustworthy.

I Used to Dream of a Day When I Would Not Feel Shame or Guilt in My Heart

I know like most of us, I have lived a life frantically rushing from one priority to another. Even now as I am ill in bed with flu. Not man-flu I hasten to add. I have often rushed from task to task so much so that the end of one task is just an invitation to start another. No gaps in between in which to take a few seconds to take stock and realise what I've just completed. Just the reverse. Living around the edges of life.

I have said to myself many times, "*What have I achieved today?*" In fact, I say that to myself about this life I have led. So driven to distraction with the desire to achieve, achieve, achieve, more, more, more. You and I both know there is an alternative, in living my purpose and practicing cultivating a sense of completeness.

I have learnt that in each moment, I can be complete. I can cope. When I stand and sing my song in the chorus of this life, when I allow myself the chance to be, when I am able to notice the difference between being and doing, I see me. I am, now.

When I am driven by comparison, when I'm fixated by achievement, the next task, I am not now. I am plagued by my perception of others' expectations of me. I end up leaving my purpose at the back door. Never living fully.

I know now I have nothing to prove. I realise not everyone will understand my path. I don't care how esteemed or successful someone is; there are things they're proud of and things they're ashamed of, and inside they wish people would see more of the former and less of the latter. Deep down, they too wish to be seen.

Finding, speaking, and living my truth hasn't been easy. In my darkest hours, from pure exhaustion to near suicide, it has seemed as if the entire world has been designed from the bottom up. But I believe living my purpose eliminates the stress and anxiety that is quite overwhelming. The troubles arise from the way we live our lives, from the labels we put on ourselves, and therefore the personas we think we must be. We all want validation; it's an intrinsic human need to feel connected to other people. And oftentimes, when we feel alone, it's because we believe we haven't proven how good we are or can be. As leaders we must master the cognitive, the emotional, the behavioural, and the spiritual dimensions of intelligence underpinning leadership. We must feel the force and live through our purpose.

Yet we find ourselves caught up in a net of how we think a mother, father, brother, sister, business owner, CEO, uncle, friend must behave. When I have accepted my feelings and thoughts and not allowed them to own me, and when I've paid attention to me and not the labels, the door is open to a radically different approach to living purposefully. It is your *My Game*. The formula really works.

I had become the world's best procrastinator, putting off what I could do today till tomorrow. I don't know how many times I have told myself I'll catch up with my sleep at the weekend. When things let up a bit, I'll do more with William. Next summer, I'll relax and take a proper holiday. Well, here it is now, Deon: the future that you promised yourself last year, last month, last week. Now is the only moment you ever really have. Living through your purpose – living intentionally – is about waking up to this. It is becoming fully aware of the life I've already got rather than the life I wish I had. It is intuitive. It is the base within us all.

Living my purpose truthfully is not an alternative version of therapy, of help. It's not a technique for understanding my past (although this can happen). Living my purpose creates a series of patterns which teach me a sense of mindfulness, and what is revealed is a penetrating yet kindly awareness of the driving forces of the real me. Gradually, the external drivers – the comparisons, the perceptions I possess of others' expectations of me, the feelings of not being good enough – dissolve of their own accord. I am less consumed by the negativity, and I move towards the things that nourish me.

I can tell you all this because I have done it myself. Living through your purpose in a mindful way has a basis in science, but that really doesn't matter; it's about experiencing it. And when life starts to become difficult or appears to fall apart, you can (as I have) remind yourself of your purpose and live it. It acts like a parachute helping you fly safely to the ground, giving you the freedom to have the impact and leave the legacy your heart desires.

I used to dream of a day when I would not feel shame or guilt in my heart. I've always lived and died with my heart even though in the past I may have guarded my feelings. I have always known this, and this is what I suggest to you in this book: know your feelings, know who you are, trust yourself, and be yourself – only then will you be trustworthy. I see me. Do you see you?

I've always longed to be a man who lives and dies with the truth of his heart. What about you?